2001 Supplement to

FEDERAL COURTS, FEDERALISM AND SEPARATION OF POWERS

CASES AND MATERIALS
Second Edition

By

Donald L. Doernberg
Professor of Law
Pace University School of Law

C. Keith Wingate
Professor of Law
University of California,
Hastings College of Law

AMERICAN CASEBOOK SERIES®

WEST GROUP
A THOMSON COMPANY

ST. PAUL, MINN., 2001

West Group has created this publication to provide you with accurate and authoritative information concerning the subject matter covered. However, this publication was not necessarily prepared by persons licensed to practice law in a particular jurisdiction. West Group is not engaged in rendering legal or other professional advice, and this publication is not a substitute for the advice of an attorney. If you require legal or other expert advice, you should seek the services of a competent attorney or other professional.

American Casebook Series, and the West Group symbol
are registered trademarks used herein under license.

COPYRIGHT © 2001 By WEST GROUP
                        610 Opperman Drive
                        P.O. Box 64526
                        St. Paul, MN 55164–0526
                        1–800–328–9352

All rights reserved
Printed in the United States of America

ISBN 0–314–26025–0

TEXT IS PRINTED ON 10% POST
CONSUMER RECYCLED PAPER

Table of Contents

	Page
TABLE OF CONTENTS	i

Chapter 1. Justiciability 1
C. Standing 1
    Friends of the Earth, Incorporated v. Laidlaw Environmental Services, (TOC), Inc. 1
    Notes and Questions 17

Chapter 5. Federal Common Law 21
C. Choosing the Applicable Law and Determining Its Content: Federal Interests or Lack Thereof 21
    1. Spontaneous Generation 21
        Semtek International Incorporated v. Lockheed Martin Corporation 21
        Notes and Questions 26
    3. Implying Private Rights of Action 27
        Alexander v. Sandoval 27
        Notes and Questions 42

Chapter 6. The Federal Forum, The Fourteenth Amendment, and the Civil Rights Act of 1871 44
B. The Fourteenth Amendment in the Remedial Scheme 44

Chapter 7. The Eleventh Amendment 46
C. Less Than Meets the Eye 46
D. Extending and Cabining the Doctrine: The Limits of Limits 47

Chapter 9. Supreme Court Review of State Court Decisions 50
C. Insulating State Decisions from Supreme Court Review 50
    1. With Substantive Law 50
        a. Adequacy, Independence and Certainty 50

Chapter 10. Federal Habeas Corpus Challenges to State Custody 52
E. Relitigating Old Claims 52
F. Raising New Claims 53
    2. New Claims Based on New Law 53
        Williams (Terry) v. Taylor 54
        Notes and Questions 77
G. Exhaustion of Remedies 81

Table of Cases

The principal cases are in bold type. Cases cited or discussed in the text are roman type. References are to pages. Cases cited in principal cases and within other quoted materials are not included.

Alexander v. Sandoval, 27
Anderson v. Creighton, 45
Ashwander v. TVA, 47
Atascadero State Hospital v. Scanlon, 48
Atherton v. FDIC, 26
Bakke v. Regents of the University of California, 43
Board of Trustees of the University of Alabama v. Garrett, 48
Boyle v. United Technologies, Inc., 26
Brady v. Maryland, 52
Bush v. Gore, 20
Bush v. Palm Beach County Canvassing Board, 50
Cage v. Louisiana, 80
Cannon v. University of Chicago, 43
Cardwell v. Greene, 52
City of Boerne v. Flores, 48
City of Los Angeles v. Lyons, 18
City of Rome v. United States, 43
Cort v. Ash, 43
Dupasseur v. Rochereau, 26
Edwards v. Carpenter, 53
Fiore v. White, 79
Fitzpatrick v. Bitzer, 49
Florida Prepaid Postsecondary Educ. Expense Bd. v. College Sav. Bank, 48
Friends of the Earth, Incorporated v. Laidlaw Environmental Services (TOC), Inc., 1
Guardians Assn. v. Civil Serv. Comm'n of New York City, 42, 43
Hans v. Louisiana, 46
Harlow v. Fitzgerald, 44, 45
Kansas v. Colorado, 46
Keeney v. Tamayo-Reyes, 52
Kimel v. Florida Board of Regents, 47, 48
Linda R.S. v. Richard D., 18, 19
Lochner v. New York, 48
Marbury v. Madison, 78
Martin v. Hunter's Lessee, 78
Michigan v. Long, 51
Minnesota v. National Tea Co., 51
Murdock v. Memphis, 50
Saucier v. Katz, 44
Schweiker v. Chilicky, 43

Semtek International Incorporated v. Lockheed Martin Corporation, 21
Slack v. McDaniel, 81
Steel Co. v. Citizens for a Better Env't, , 19
Strickland v. Washington, 78
Sullivan v. Louisiana, 80
Thompson v. Thompson, 43
Tyler v. Cain, 80
Vermont Agency of Natural Resources v. United States ex rel. Stevens, 47
Williams (Michael) v. Taylor, 52
Williams (Terry) v. Taylor, 54

Chapter 1

JUSTICIABILITY

C. STANDING

To be added at page 102, before "D. Ripeness":

**FRIENDS OF THE EARTH, INCORPORATED v.
LAIDLAW ENVIRONMENTAL SERVICES (TOC), INC.**
Supreme Court of the United States, 2000.
528 U.S. 167, 120 S.Ct. 693, 145 L.Ed.2d 610.

JUSTICE GINSBURG delivered the opinion of the Court.

This case presents an important question concerning the operation of the citizen-suit provisions of the Clean Water Act. Congress authorized the federal district courts to entertain Clean Water Act suits initiated by "a person or persons having an interest which is or may be adversely affected." To impel future compliance with the Act, a district court may prescribe injunctive relief in such a suit; additionally or alternatively, the court may impose civil penalties payable to the United States Treasury. In the Clean Water Act citizen suit now before us, the District Court determined that injunctive relief was inappropriate because the defendant, after the institution of the litigation, achieved substantial compliance with the terms of its discharge permit. The court did, however, assess a civil penalty of $405,800. The "total deterrent effect" of the penalty would be adequate to forestall future violations, the court reasoned, taking into account that the defendant "will be required to reimburse plaintiffs for a significant amount of legal fees and has, itself, incurred significant legal expenses."

The Court of Appeals vacated the District Court's order. The case became moot, the appellate court declared, once the defendant fully complied with the terms of its permit and the plaintiff failed to appeal the denial of equitable relief. "[C]ivil penalties payable to the government," the Court of Appeals stated, "would not redress any injury Plaintiffs have suffered." Nor were attorneys' fees in order, the Court of Appeals noted, because absent relief on the merits, plaintiffs could not qualify as prevailing parties.

We reverse the judgment of the Court of Appeals. The appellate court erred in concluding that a citizen suitor's claim for civil penalties must be dismissed as moot when the defendant, albeit after commencement of the litigation, has come into compliance. In directing dismissal of the suit on grounds of mootness, the Court of Appeals incorrectly conflated our case law on initial standing to bring suit with our case law on post-commencement mootness. A defendant's voluntary cessation of allegedly unlawful conduct ordinarily does not suffice to moot a case. The Court of Appeals also misperceived the remedial potential of civil penalties. Such penalties may serve, as an alternative to an injunction, to deter future violations and thereby redress the injuries that prompted a citizen suitor to commence litigation.

I

A

In 1972, Congress enacted the Clean Water Act (Act) * * * . 33 U.S.C. § 1342 provides for the issuance, by the Administrator of the Environmental Protection Agency (EPA) or by authorized States, of National Pollutant Discharge Elimination System (NPDES) permits. NPDES permits impose limitations on the discharge of pollutants, and establish related monitoring and reporting requirements, in order to improve the cleanliness and safety of the Nation's waters. Noncompliance with a permit constitutes a violation of the Act. § 1342(h).

* * * [A] suit to enforce any limitation in an NPDES permit may be brought by any "citizen," defined as "a person or persons having an interest which is or may be adversely affected." Sixty days before initiating a citizen suit, however, the would-be plaintiff must give notice of the alleged violation to the EPA, the State in which the alleged violation occurred, and the alleged violator. "[T]he purpose of notice to the alleged violator is to give it an opportunity to bring itself into complete compliance with the Act and thus * * * render unnecessary a citizen suit." Accordingly, we have held that citizens lack statutory standing under § 505(a) to sue for violations that have ceased by the time the complaint is filed. The Act also bars a citizen from suing if the EPA or the State has already commenced, and is "diligently prosecuting," an enforcement action.

The Act authorizes district courts in citizen-suit proceedings to enter injunctions and to assess civil penalties, which are payable to the United States Treasury. In determining the amount of any civil penalty, the district court must take into account "the seriousness of the violation or violations, the economic benefit (if any) resulting from the violation, any history of such violations, any good-faith efforts to comply with the applicable requirements, the economic impact of the penalty on the violator, and such other matters as justice may require." In addition, the court "may award costs of litigation (including reasonable attorney and expert witness fees) to any prevailing or substantially prevailing party, whenever the court determines such award is appropriate."

B

In 1986, defendant-respondent Laidlaw Environmental Services (TOC), Inc., bought a hazardous waste incinerator facility in Roebuck, South Carolina, that included a wastewater treatment plant. * * * Shortly after Laidlaw acquired the facility, the South Carolina Department of Health and Environmental Control (DHEC) * * * granted Laidlaw an NPDES permit authorizing the company to discharge treated water into the North Tyger River. The permit, which became effective on January 1, 1987, placed limits on Laidlaw's discharge of several pollutants into the river, including—of particular relevance to this case—mercury, an extremely toxic pollutant. The permit also regulated the flow, temperature, toxicity, and pH of the effluent from the facility, and imposed monitoring and reporting obligations.

Once it received its permit, Laidlaw began to discharge various pollutants into the waterway; repeatedly, Laidlaw's discharges exceeded the limits set by the permit. In particular, despite experimenting with several technological fixes, Laidlaw consistently failed to meet the permit's stringent 1.3 ppb (parts per billion) daily average limit on mercury discharges. The District Court later found that Laidlaw had violated the mercury limits on 489 occasions between 1987 and 1995.

On April 10, 1992, plaintiff-petitioners Friends of the Earth (FOE) and Citizens Local Environmental Action Network, Inc. (CLEAN) (referred to collectively in this opinion, together with later joined plaintiff-petitioner Sierra Club, as "FOE") took the preliminary step necessary to the institution of litigation. They sent a letter to Laidlaw notifying the company of their intention to file a citizen suit against it * * * after the expiration of the requisite 60-day notice period, *i.e.*, on or after June 10, 1992. Laidlaw's lawyer then contacted DHEC to ask whether DHEC would consider filing a lawsuit against Laidlaw. The District Court later found that Laidlaw's reason for requesting that DHEC file a lawsuit against it was to bar FOE's proposed citizen suit through the operation of 33 U.S.C. § 1365(b)(1)(B). DHEC agreed to file a lawsuit against Laidlaw; the company's lawyer then drafted the complaint for DHEC and paid the filing fee. On June 9, 1992, the last day before FOE's 60-day notice period expired, DHEC and Laidlaw reached a settlement requiring Laidlaw to pay $100,000 in civil penalties and to make " 'every effort' " to comply with its permit obligations.

On June 12, 1992, FOE filed this citizen suit against Laidlaw under § 505(a) of the Act, alleging noncompliance with the NPDES permit and seeking declaratory and injunctive relief and an award of civil penalties. Laidlaw moved for summary judgment on the ground that FOE had failed to present evidence demonstrating injury in fact, and therefore lacked Article III standing to bring the lawsuit. In opposition to this motion, FOE submitted affidavits and deposition testimony from members of the plaintiff organizations. The record before the District Court also included affidavits from the organizations' members submitted by FOE in support of an earlier motion for preliminary injunctive relief. After examining this evidence, the District Court denied Laidlaw's summary judgment motion, finding—albeit "by the very slimmest of margins"—that FOE had standing to bring the suit.

Laidlaw also moved to dismiss the action on the ground that the citizen suit was barred * * * by DHEC's prior action against the company. The United States, appearing as *amicus curiae*, joined FOE in opposing the motion. After an extensive analysis of the Laidlaw-DHEC settlement and the circumstances under which it was reached, the District Court held that DHEC's action against Laidlaw had not been "diligently prosecuted"; consequently, the court allowed FOE's citizen suit to proceed.[1] The record indicates that after FOE initiated the suit, but before the District Court rendered judgment, Laidlaw violated the mercury discharge limitation in its permit 13 times. The District Court also found that Laidlaw had committed 13 monitoring and 10 reporting violations during this period. The last recorded mercury discharge violation occurred in January 1995, long after the complaint was filed but about two years before judgment was rendered.

On January 22, 1997, the District Court * * * found that Laidlaw had gained a total economic benefit of $1,092,581 as a result of its extended period of noncompliance with the mercury discharge limit in its permit. The court concluded, however, that a civil penalty of $405,800 was adequate in light of the guiding factors listed in 33 U.S.C. § 1319(d). In particular, the District Court stated that the lesser penalty was appropriate taking into account the judgment's "total deterrent effect." In reaching this determination, the court "considered that Laidlaw will be required to reimburse plaintiffs for a significant amount of legal fees." The court declined to grant FOE's request for injunctive relief, stating that an injunction was inappropriate because "Laidlaw has been in substantial compliance with all parameters in its NPDES permit since at least August 1992."

FOE appealed the District Court's civil penalty judgment, arguing that the penalty was inadequate, but did not appeal the denial of declaratory or injunctive relief. Laidlaw cross-appealed, arguing, among other things, that FOE lacked standing to bring the suit and that DHEC's action qualified as a diligent prosecution precluding FOE's litigation. The United States continued to participate as *amicus curiae* in support of FOE.

* * * The Court of Appeals assumed without deciding that FOE initially had standing to bring the action, but went on to hold that the case had become moot. The appellate court stated, first, that the elements of Article III standing—injury, causation, and redressability—must persist at every stage of review, or else the action becomes moot. Citing our decision in *Steel Co.*, the Court of Appeals reasoned that the case had become moot because "the only remedy currently available to [FOE]—civil penalties payable to the government—would not redress any injury [FOE has] suffered." The court therefore vacated the District Court's order and remanded with instructions to dismiss the action. In a footnote, the Court of Appeals added that FOE's "failure to obtain relief on the merits of [its] claims precludes any recovery of attorneys' fees or other litigation costs because such an award is available only to a 'prevailing or substantially prevailing party.' "

According to Laidlaw, after the Court of Appeals issued its decision but before this Court granted certiorari, the entire incinerator facility in Roebuck was permanently closed, dismantled, and put up for sale, and all discharges from the

---

[1] The District Court noted that "Laidlaw drafted the state—court complaint and settlement agreement, filed the lawsuit against itself, and paid the filing fee." Further, "the settlement agreement between DHEC and Laidlaw was entered into with unusual haste, without giving the Plaintiffs the opportunity to intervene." The court found "most persuasive" the fact that "in imposing the civil penalty of $100,000 against Laidlaw, DHEC failed to recover, or even to calculate, the economic benefit that Laidlaw received by not complying with its permit."

facility permanently ceased.

We granted certiorari to resolve the inconsistency between the Fourth Circuit's decision in this case and the decisions of several other Courts of Appeals, which have held that a defendant's compliance with its permit after the commencement of litigation does not moot claims for civil penalties under the Act.

II

A

The Constitution's case-or-controversy limitation on federal judicial authority underpins both our standing and our mootness jurisprudence, but the two inquiries differ in respects critical to the proper resolution of this case, so we address them separately. Because the Court of Appeals was persuaded that the case had become moot and so held, it simply assumed without deciding that FOE had initial standing. But because we hold that the Court of Appeals erred in declaring the case moot, we have an obligation to assure ourselves that FOE had Article III standing at the outset of the litigation. We therefore address the question of standing before turning to mootness.

In *Lujan v. Defenders of Wildlife* we held that, to satisfy Article III's standing requirements, a plaintiff must show (1) it has suffered an "injury in fact" that is (a) concrete and particularized and (b) actual or imminent, not conjectural or hypothetical; (2) the injury is fairly traceable to the challenged action of the defendant; and (3) it is likely, as opposed to merely speculative, that the injury will be redressed by a favorable decision. An association has standing to bring suit on behalf of its members when its members would otherwise have standing to sue in their own right, the interests at stake are germane to the organization's purpose, and neither the claim asserted nor the relief requested requires the participation of individual members in the lawsuit.

Laidlaw contends first that FOE lacked standing from the outset even to seek injunctive relief, because the plaintiff organizations failed to show that any of their members had sustained or faced the threat of any "injury in fact" from Laidlaw's activities. In support of this contention Laidlaw points to the District Court's finding, made in the course of setting the penalty amount, that there had been "no demonstrated proof of harm to the environment" from Laidlaw's mercury discharge violations.

The relevant showing for purposes of Article III standing, however, is not injury to the environment but injury to the plaintiff. To insist upon the former rather than the latter as part of the standing inquiry (as the dissent in essence does) is to raise the standing hurdle higher than the necessary showing for success on the merits in an action alleging noncompliance with an NPDES permit. Focusing properly on injury to the plaintiff, the District Court found that FOE had demonstrated sufficient injury to establish standing. For example, FOE member Kenneth Lee Curtis averred in affidavits that he lived a half-mile from Laidlaw's facility; that he occasionally drove over the North Tyger River, and that it looked and smelled polluted; and that he would like to fish, camp, swim, and picnic in and near the river between 3 and 15 miles downstream from the facility, as he did when he was a teenager, but would not do so because he was concerned that the water was polluted by Laidlaw's discharges. Curtis reaffirmed these statements in extensive deposition testimony. For example, he testified that he would like to fish in the river at a specific spot he used as a boy, but that he would not do so now because of his concerns about Laidlaw's discharges.

Other members presented evidence to similar effect. CLEAN member Angela Patterson attested that she lived two miles from the facility; that before Laidlaw operated the facility, she picnicked, walked, birdwatched, and waded in and along the North Tyger River because of the natural beauty of the area; that she no longer engaged in these activities in or near the river because she was concerned about harmful effects from discharged pollutants; and that she and her husband would like to purchase a home near the river but did not intend to do so, in part because of Laidlaw's discharges. CLEAN member Judy Pruitt averred that she lived one-quarter mile from Laidlaw's facility and would like to fish, hike, and picnic along the North Tyger River, but has refrained from those activities because of the discharges. FOE member Linda Moore attested that she lived 20 miles from Roebuck, and would use the North Tyger River south of Roebuck and the land surrounding it for recreational purposes were she not concerned that the water contained harmful pollutants. In her deposition, Moore testified at length that she would hike, picnic, camp, swim, boat, and drive near or in the river were it not for her concerns about illegal discharges. CLEAN member Gail Lee attested that her home, which is near Laidlaw's facility, had a lower value than similar homes located further from the facility, and that she believed the pollutant discharges accounted for some of the discrepancy. Sierra Club member Norman Sharp averred that he had canoed approximately 40 miles downstream of the Laidlaw facility and would like to canoe in the North Tyger River closer to Laidlaw's discharge point, but did not do so because he was concerned that the water contained harmful pollutants.

These sworn statements, as the District Court determined, adequately documented injury in fact. We have held that environmental plaintiffs adequately allege injury in fact when they aver that they use the affected area and are persons "for whom the aesthetic and recreational values of the area will be lessened" by the challenged activity.

* * * *Lujan* is not to the contrary. In that case an environmental organization assailed the Bureau of Land Management's "land withdrawal review program," a program covering millions of acres, alleging that the program illegally opened up public lands to mining activities. The defendants moved for summary judgment, challenging the plaintiff organization's standing to initiate the action under the Administrative Procedure Act. We held that the plaintiff could not survive the summary judgment motion merely by offering "averments which state only that one of [the organization's] members uses unspecified portions of an immense tract of territory, on some portions of which mining activity has occurred or probably will occur by virtue of the governmental action."

In contrast, the affidavits and testimony presented by FOE in this case assert that Laidlaw's discharges, and the affiant members' reasonable concerns about the effects of those discharges, directly affected those affiants' recreational, aesthetic, and economic interests. These submissions present dispositively more than the mere "general averments" and "conclusory allegations" found inadequate in [*Lujan*]. Nor can the affiants' conditional statements—that they would use the nearby North Tyger River for recreation if Laidlaw were not discharging pollutants into it—be equated with the speculative " 'some day' intentions" to visit endangered species halfway around the world that we held insufficient to show injury in fact in [*Lujan*].

Los Angeles v. Lyons, relied on by the dissent, does not weigh against standing in this case. In *Lyons*, we held that a plaintiff lacked standing to seek an injunction against the enforcement of a police chokehold policy because he could not credibly allege that he faced a realistic threat from the policy. In the footnote from *Lyons* cited by the dissent, we noted that "[t]he reasonableness of Lyons' fear is dependent upon the likelihood of a recurrence of the allegedly unlawful conduct," and that his "subjective apprehensions" that such a recurrence would even take place were not enough to support standing. Here, in contrast, it is undisputed that Laidlaw's unlawful conduct— discharging pollutants in excess of permit limits—was occurring at the time the complaint was filed. Under *Lyons*, then, the only "subjective" issue here is "[t]he reasonableness of [the] fear" that led the affiants to respond to that concededly ongoing conduct by refraining from use of the North Tyger River and surrounding areas. Unlike the dissent, we see nothing "improbable" about the proposition that a company's continuous and pervasive illegal discharges of pollutants into a river would cause nearby residents to curtail their recreational use of that waterway and would subject them to other economic and aesthetic harms. * * * [T]he District Court found it was true in this case, and that is enough for injury in fact.

Laidlaw argues next that even if FOE had standing to seek injunctive relief, it lacked standing to seek civil penalties. Here the asserted defect is not injury but redressability. Civil penalties offer no redress to private plaintiffs, Laidlaw argues, because they are paid to the government, and therefore a citizen plaintiff can never have standing to seek them.

Laidlaw is right to insist that a plaintiff must demonstrate standing separately for each form of relief sought. But it is wrong to maintain that citizen plaintiffs facing ongoing violations never have standing to seek civil penalties.

We have recognized on numerous occasions that "all civil penalties have some deterrent effect." More specifically, Congress has found that civil penalties in Clean Water Act cases do more than promote immediate compliance by limiting the defendant's economic incentive to delay its attainment of permit limits; they also deter future violations. This congressional determination warrants judicial attention and respect. "The legislative history of the Act reveals that Congress wanted the district court to consider the need for retribution and deterrence, in addition to restitution, when it imposed civil penalties. * * * [The district court may] seek to deter future violations by basing the penalty on its economic impact."

It can scarcely be doubted that, for a plaintiff who is injured or faces the threat of future injury due to illegal conduct ongoing at the time of suit, a sanction that effectively abates that conduct and prevents its recurrence provides a form of redress. Civil penalties can fit that description. To the extent that they encourage defendants to discontinue current violations and deter them from committing future ones, they afford redress to citizen plaintiffs who are injured or threatened with injury as a consequence of ongoing unlawful conduct.

The dissent argues that it is the availability rather than the imposition of civil penalties that deters any particular polluter from continuing to pollute. This argument misses the mark in two ways. First, it overlooks the interdependence of the availability and the imposition; a threat has no deterrent value unless it is credible that it will be carried out. Second, it is reasonable for Congress to conclude that an actual award of civil penalties does in fact bring with it a significant quantum of deterrence over and above what is achieved by the mere prospect of such penalties. A would-be polluter may or may not be dissuaded by the existence of a remedy on the books, but a defendant once hit in its pocketbook will surely think twice before polluting again.[2]

We recognize that there may be a point at which the deterrent effect of a claim for civil penalties becomes so insubstantial or so remote that it cannot support citizen standing. The fact that this vanishing point is not easy to ascertain does not detract from the deterrent power of such penalties in the ordinary case. Justice Frankfurter's observations for the Court, made in a different context nearly 60 years ago, hold true here as well:

> How to effectuate policy—the adaptation of means to legitimately sought ends—is one of the most intractable of legislative problems. Whether proscribed conduct is to be deterred by qui tam action or triple damages or injunction, or by criminal prosecution, or merely by defense to actions in contract, or by some, or all, of these remedies in combination, is a matter within the legislature's range of choice. Judgment on the deterrent effect of the various weapons in the armory of the law can lay little claim to scientific basis.

In this case we need not explore the outer limits of the principle that civil penalties provide sufficient deterrence to support redressability. Here, the civil penalties sought by FOE carried with them a deterrent effect that made it likely, as opposed to merely speculative, that the penalties would redress FOE's injuries by abating current violations and preventing future ones—as the District Court reasonably found when it assessed a penalty of $405,800.

Laidlaw contends that the reasoning of our decision in *Steel Co.* directs the conclusion that citizen plaintiffs have no standing to seek civil penalties under the Act. We disagree. *Steel Co.* established that citizen suitors lack standing to seek civil penalties for violations that have abated by the time of suit. We specifically noted in that case that there was no allegation in the complaint of any

---

[2] The dissent suggests that there was little deterrent work for civil penalties to do in this case because the lawsuit brought against Laidlaw by DHEC had already pushed the level of deterrence to "near the top of the graph." This suggestion ignores the District Court's specific finding that the penalty agreed to by Laidlaw and DHEC was far too low to remove Laidlaw's economic benefit from noncompliance, and thus was inadequate to deter future violations. And it begins to look especially farfetched when one recalls that Laidlaw itself prompted the DHEC lawsuit, paid the filing fee, and drafted the complaint.

continuing or imminent violation, and that no basis for such an allegation appeared to exist. In short, *Steel Co.* held that private plaintiffs, unlike the Federal Government, may not sue to assess penalties for wholly past violations, but our decision in that case did not reach the issue of standing to seek penalties for violations that are ongoing at the time of the complaint and that could continue into the future if undeterred.[4]

B

Satisfied that FOE had standing under Article III to bring this action, we turn to the question of mootness.

The only conceivable basis for a finding of mootness in this case is Laidlaw's voluntary conduct—either its achievement by August 1992 of substantial compliance with its NPDES permit or its more recent shutdown of the Roebuck facility. It is well settled that "a defendant's voluntary cessation of a challenged practice does not deprive a federal court of its power to determine the legality of the practice." "[I]f it did, the courts would be compelled to leave '[t]he defendant * * * free to return to his old ways.'" In accordance with this principle, the standard we have announced for determining whether a case has been mooted by the defendant's voluntary conduct is stringent: "A case might become moot if subsequent events made it absolutely clear that the allegedly wrongful behavior could not reasonably be expected to recur." The "heavy burden of persua[ding]" the court that the challenged conduct cannot reasonably be expected to start up again lies with the party asserting mootness.

The Court of Appeals justified its mootness disposition by reference to *Steel Co.*, which held that citizen plaintiffs lack standing to seek civil penalties for wholly past violations. In relying on *Steel Co.*, the Court of Appeals confused mootness with standing. The confusion is understandable, given this

---

[4] In insisting that the redressability requirement is not met, the dissent relies heavily on *Linda R.S. v. Richard D.* That reliance is sorely misplaced. In *Linda R. S.*, the mother of an out-of-wedlock child filed suit to force a district attorney to bring a criminal prosecution against the absentee father for failure to pay child support. In finding that the mother lacked standing to seek this extraordinary remedy, the Court drew attention to "the special status of criminal prosecutions in our system" and carefully limited its holding to the "unique context of a challenge to [the non-enforcement of] a criminal statute." Furthermore, as to redressability, the relief sought in *Linda R. S.*—a prosecution which, if successful, would automatically land the delinquent father in jail for a fixed term, with predictably negative effects on his earning power—would scarcely remedy the plaintiff's lack of child support payments. In this regard, the Court contrasted "the civil contempt model whereby the defendant 'keeps the keys to the jail in his own pocket' and may be released whenever he complies with his legal obligations." The dissent's contention, that "precisely the same situation exists here" as in *Linda R. S.* is, to say the least, extravagant.

Putting aside its mistaken reliance on *Linda R. S.*, the dissent's broader charge that citizen suits for civil penalties under the Act carry "grave implications for democratic governance" seems to us overdrawn. Certainly the federal Executive Branch does not share the dissent's view that such suits dissipate its authority to enforce the law. In fact, the Department of Justice has endorsed this citizen suit from the outset, submitting *amicus* briefs in support of FOE in the District Court, the Court of Appeals, and this Court. As we have already noted, the Federal Government retains the power to foreclose a citizen suit by undertaking its own action. And if the Executive Branch opposes a particular citizen suit, the statute allows the Administrator of the EPA to "intervene as a matter of right" and bring the Government's views to the attention of the court.

Court's repeated statements that the doctrine of mootness can be described as "the doctrine of standing set in a time frame: The requisite personal interest that must exist at the commencement of the litigation (standing) must continue throughout its existence (mootness)."

Careful reflection on the long-recognized exceptions to mootness, however, reveals that the description of mootness as "standing set in a time frame" is not comprehensive. As just noted, a defendant claiming that its voluntary compliance moots a case bears the formidable burden of showing that it is absolutely clear the allegedly wrongful behavior could not reasonably be expected to recur. By contrast, in a lawsuit brought to force compliance, it is the plaintiff's burden to establish standing by demonstrating that, if unchecked by the litigation, the defendant's allegedly wrongful behavior will likely occur or continue, and that the "threatened injury [is] certainly impending." Thus, in *Lyons*, as already noted, we held that a plaintiff lacked initial standing to seek an injunction against the enforcement of a police chokehold policy because he could not credibly allege that he faced a realistic threat arising from the policy. Elsewhere in the opinion, however, we noted that a citywide moratorium on police chokeholds—an action that surely diminished the already slim likelihood that any particular individual would be choked by police—would not have mooted an otherwise valid claim for injunctive relief, because the moratorium by its terms was not permanent. The plain lesson of these cases is that there are circumstances in which the prospect that a defendant will engage in (or resume) harmful conduct may be too speculative to support standing, but not too speculative to overcome mootness.

Furthermore, if mootness were simply "standing set in a time frame," the exception to mootness that arises when the defendant's allegedly unlawful activity is "capable of repetition, yet evading review" could not exist. * * * Standing admits of no similar exception; if a plaintiff lacks standing at the time the action commences, the fact that the dispute is capable of repetition yet evading review will not entitle the complainant to a federal judicial forum.

We acknowledged the distinction between mootness and standing most recently in *Steel Co.*:

> The United States * * * argues that the injunctive relief does constitute remediation because "there is a presumption of [future] injury when the defendant has voluntarily ceased its illegal activity in response to litigation," even if that occurs before a complaint is filed * * *. This makes a sword out of a shield. The "presumption" the Government refers to has been applied to refute the assertion of mootness by a defendant who, when sued in a complaint that alleges present or threatened injury, ceases the complained-of activity* * * . It is an immense and unacceptable stretch to call the presumption into service as a substitute for the allegation of present or threatened injury upon which initial standing must be based.

Standing doctrine functions to ensure, among other things, that the scarce resources of the federal courts are devoted to those disputes in which the parties have a concrete stake. In contrast, by the time mootness is an issue, the case has been brought and litigated, often (as here) for years. To abandon the case at an advanced stage may prove more wasteful than frugal. This argument from sunk costs does not license courts to retain jurisdiction over cases in which one or both of the parties plainly lacks a continuing interest, as when the parties have settled or a plaintiff pursuing a nonsurviving claim has died. But the argument surely highlights an important difference between the two doctrines.

In its brief, Laidlaw appears to argue that, regardless of the effect of Laidlaw's compliance, FOE doomed its own civil penalty claim to mootness by failing to appeal the District Court's denial of injunctive relief. This argument misconceives the statutory scheme. * * * [T]he district court has discretion to determine which form of relief is best suited, in the particular case, to abate current violations and deter future ones. "[A] federal judge sitting as chancellor is not mechanically obligated to grant an injunction for every violation of law." Denial of injunctive relief does not necessarily mean that the district court has concluded there is no prospect of future violations for civil penalties to deter. Indeed, it meant no such thing in this case. The District Court denied injunctive relief, but expressly based its award of civil penalties on the need for deterrence. As the dissent notes, federal courts should aim to ensure " 'the framing of relief no broader than required by the precise facts.' " In accordance with this aim, a district court in a Clean Water Act citizen suit properly may conclude that an injunction would be an excessively intrusive remedy, because it could entail continuing superintendence of the permit holder's activities by a federal court—a process burdensome to court and permit holder alike.

Laidlaw also asserts, in a supplemental suggestion of mootness, that the closure of its Roebuck facility, which took place after the Court of Appeals issued its decision, mooted the case. The facility closure, like Laidlaw's earlier achievement of substantial compliance with its permit requirements, might moot the case, but—we once more reiterate—only if one or the other of these events made it absolutely clear that Laidlaw's permit violations could not reasonably be expected to recur. The effect of both Laidlaw's compliance and the facility closure on the prospect of future violations is a disputed factual matter. FOE points out, for example—and Laidlaw does not appear to contest—that Laidlaw retains its NPDES permit. These issues have not been aired in the lower courts; they remain open for consideration on remand.

C

[The Court's declined to discuss whether plaintiffs were entitled to attorney's fees, since the district court, though indicating that it might award fees, had delayed its final decision until final appellate disposition of the case.]

* * *

For the reasons stated, the judgment of the United States Court of Appeals for the Fourth Circuit is reversed, and the case is remanded for further proceedings consistent with this opinion.

It is so ordered.

JUSTICE STEVENS, concurring.

Although the Court has identified a sufficient reason for rejecting the Court of Appeals' mootness determination, it is important also to note that the case would not be moot even if it were absolutely clear that respondent had gone out of business and posed no threat of future permit violations. The District Court entered a valid judgment requiring respondent to pay a civil penalty of $405,800 to the United States. No post-judgment conduct of respondent could retroactively invalidate that judgment. A record of voluntary post-judgment compliance that would justify a decision that injunctive relief is unnecessary, or even a decision that any claim for injunctive relief is now moot, would not warrant vacation of the valid money judgment.

Furthermore, petitioners' claim for civil penalties would not be moot even if it were absolutely clear that respondent's violations could not reasonably be expected to recur because respondent achieved substantial compliance with its permit requirements after petitioners filed their complaint but before the District Court entered judgment. As the Courts of Appeals (other than the court below) have uniformly concluded, a polluter's voluntary post-complaint cessation of an alleged violation will not moot a citizen-suit claim for civil penalties even if it is sufficient to moot a related claim for injunctive or declaratory relief. This conclusion is consistent with the structure of the Clean Water Act, which attaches liability for civil penalties at the time a permit violation occurs. It is also consistent with the character of civil penalties, which, for purposes of mootness analysis, should be equated with punitive damages rather than with injunctive or declaratory relief. No one contends that a defendant's post-complaint conduct could moot a claim for punitive damages; civil penalties should be treated the same way.

The cases cited by the Court in its discussion of the mootness issue all involved requests for injunctive or declaratory relief. In only * * * *Los Angeles v. Lyons* did the plaintiff seek damages, and in that case the opinion makes it clear that the inability to obtain injunctive relief would have no impact on the damages claim. There is no precedent, either in our jurisprudence, or in any other of which I am aware, that provides any support for the suggestion that post-complaint factual developments that might moot a claim for injunctive or declaratory relief could either moot a claim for monetary relief or retroactively invalidate a valid money judgment.

JUSTICE SCALIA, with whom JUSTICE THOMAS joins, dissenting.

The Court begins its analysis by finding injury in fact on the basis of vague affidavits that are undermined by the District Court's express finding that Laidlaw's discharges caused no demonstrable harm to the environment. It then proceeds to marry private wrong with public remedy in a union that violates traditional principles of federal standing—thereby permitting law enforcement to be placed in the hands of private individuals. Finally, the Court suggests that to avoid mootness one needs even less of a stake in the outcome than the Court's watered-down requirements for initial standing. I dissent from all of this.

I

Plaintiffs, as the parties invoking federal jurisdiction, have the burden of proof and persuasion as to the existence of standing. The plaintiffs in this case fell far short of carrying their burden of demonstrating injury in fact. The Court cites affiants' testimony asserting that their enjoyment of the North Tyger River has been diminished due to "concern" that the water was polluted, and that they "believed" that Laidlaw's mercury exceedances had reduced the value of their homes. These averments alone cannot carry the plaintiffs' burden of demonstrating that they have suffered a "concrete and particularized" injury. General allegations of injury may suffice at the pleading stage, but at summary judgment plaintiffs must set forth "specific facts" to support their claims. And where, as here, the case has proceeded to judgment, those specific facts must be " 'supported adequately by the evidence adduced at trial.' " In this case, the affidavits themselves are woefully short on "specific facts," and the vague allegations of injury they do make are undermined by the evidence adduced at trial.

Typically, an environmental plaintiff claiming injury due to discharges in violation of the Clean Water Act argues that the discharges harm the environment, and that the harm to the environment injures him. This route to injury is barred in the present case, however, since the District Court concluded after considering all the evidence that there had been "no demonstrated proof of harm to the environment," , that the "permit violations at issue in this citizen suit did not result in any health risk or environmental harm," that "[a]ll available data * * * fail to show that Laidlaw's actual discharges have resulted in harm to the North Tyger River," and that "the overall quality of the river exceeds levels necessary to support * * * recreation in and on the water."

The Court finds these conclusions unproblematic for standing, because "[t]he relevant showing for purposes of Article III standing * * * is not injury to the environment but injury to the plaintiff." This statement is correct, as far as it goes. We have certainly held that a demonstration of harm to the environment is not enough to satisfy the injury-in-fact requirement unless the plaintiff can demonstrate how he personally was harmed. In the normal course, however, a lack of demonstrable harm to the environment will translate, as it plainly does here, into a lack of demonstrable harm to citizen plaintiffs. While it is perhaps possible that a plaintiff could be harmed even though the environment was not, such a plaintiff would have the burden of articulating and demonstrating the nature of that injury. Ongoing "concerns" about the environment are not enough, for "[i]t is the reality of the threat of repeated injury that is relevant to the standing inquiry, not the plaintiff's subjective apprehensions." *Los Angeles v. Lyons*. At the very least, in the present case, one would expect to see evidence supporting the affidavits' bald assertions regarding decreasing recreational usage and declining home values, as well as evidence for the improbable proposition that Laidlaw's violations, even though harmless to the environment, are somehow responsible for these effects. Plaintiffs here have made no attempt at such a showing, but rely entirely upon unsupported and unexplained affidavit allegations of "concern."

Indeed, every one of the affiants deposed by Laidlaw cast into doubt the (in any event inadequate) proposition that subjective "concerns" actually affected their conduct. Linda Moore, for example, said in her affidavit that she would use the affected waterways for recreation if it were not for her concern about pollution. Yet she testified in her deposition that she had been to the river only twice, once in 1980 (when she visited someone who lived by the river) and once after this suit was filed. Similarly, Kenneth Lee Curtis, who claimed he was injured by being deprived of recreational activity at the river, admitted that he had not been to the river since he was "a kid," and when asked whether the reason he stopped visiting the river was because of pollution, answered "no." As to Curtis's claim that the river "looke[d] and smell[ed] polluted," this condition, if present, was surely not caused by Laidlaw's discharges, which according to the District Court "did not result in any health risk or environmental harm." The other affiants cited by the Court were not deposed, but their affidavits state either that they would use the river if it were not polluted or harmful (as the court subsequently found it is not), or said that the river looks polluted (which is also incompatible with the court's findings). These affiants have established nothing but "subjective apprehensions."

The Court is correct that the District Court explicitly found standing—albeit "by the very slimmest of margins," and as "an awfully close call." That cautious finding, however, was made in 1993, long before the court's 1997 conclusion that Laidlaw's discharges did not harm the environment. As we have previously recognized, an initial conclusion that plaintiffs have standing is subject to reexamination, particularly if later evidence proves inconsistent with that conclusion. Laidlaw challenged the existence of injury in fact on appeal to the Fourth Circuit, but that court did not reach the question. Thus no lower court has reviewed the injury-in-fact issue in light of the extensive studies that led the District Court to conclude that the environment was not harmed by Laidlaw's discharges.

Inexplicably, the Court is untroubled by this, but proceeds to find injury in fact in the most casual fashion, as though it is merely confirming a careful analysis made below. Although we have previously refused to find standing based on the "conclusory allegations of an affidavit," the Court is content to do just that today. By accepting plaintiffs' vague, contradictory, and unsubstantiated allegations of "concern" about the environment as adequate to prove injury in fact, and accepting them even in the face of a finding that the environment was not demonstrably harmed, the Court makes the injury-in-fact requirement a sham. If there are permit violations, and a member of a plaintiff environmental organization lives near the offending plant, it would be difficult not to satisfy today's lenient standard.

II

The Court's treatment of the redressability requirement—which would have been unnecessary if it resolved the injury-in-fact question correctly—is equally cavalier. As discussed above, petitioners allege ongoing injury consisting of diminished enjoyment of the affected waterways and decreased property values. They allege that these injuries are caused by Laidlaw's continuing permit violations. But the remedy petitioners seek is neither recompense for their injuries nor an injunction against future violations. Instead, the remedy is a statutorily specified "penalty" for past violations, payable entirely to the United States Treasury. Only last Term, we held that such penalties do not redress any injury a citizen plaintiff has suffered from past violations. The Court nonetheless finds the redressability requirement satisfied here, distinguishing *Steel Co.* on the ground that in this case the petitioners allege ongoing violations; payment of the penalties, it says, will remedy petitioners' injury by deterring future violations by Laidlaw. It holds that a penalty payable to the public "remedies" a threatened private harm, and suffices to sustain a private suit.

That holding has no precedent in our jurisprudence, and takes this Court beyond the "cases and controversies" that Article III of the Constitution has entrusted to its resolution. Even if it were appropriate, moreover, to allow Article III's remediation requirement to be satisfied by the indirect private consequences of a public penalty, those consequences are entirely too speculative in the present case. The new standing law that the Court makes—like all expansions of standing beyond the traditional constitutional limits—has grave implications for democratic governance. I shall discuss these three points in turn.

A

* * *

* * * The principle that "in American jurisprudence * * * a private citizen lacks a judicially cognizable interest in the prosecution or nonprosecution of another" applies no less to prosecution for civil penalties payable to the State than to prosecution for criminal penalties owing to the State.

The Court's opinion reads as though the only purpose and effect of the redressability requirement is to assure that the plaintiff receive some of the benefit of the relief that a court orders. That is not so. If it were, a federal tort plaintiff fearing repetition of the injury could ask for tort damages to be paid, not only to himself but to other victims as well, on the theory that those damages would have at least some deterrent effect beneficial to him. Such a suit is preposterous because the "remediation" that is the traditional business of Anglo-American courts is relief specifically tailored to the plaintiff's injury, and not any sort of relief that has some incidental benefit to the plaintiff. Just as a "generalized grievance" that affects the entire citizenry cannot satisfy the injury-in-fact requirement even though it aggrieves the plaintiff along with everyone else, so also a generalized remedy that deters all future unlawful activity against all persons cannot satisfy the remediation requirement, even though it deters (among other things) repetition of this particular unlawful activity against these particular plaintiffs.

Thus, relief against prospective harm is traditionally afforded by way of an injunction, the scope of which is limited by the scope of the threatened injury. In seeking to overturn that tradition by giving an individual plaintiff the power to invoke a public remedy, Congress has done precisely what we have said it cannot do: convert an "undifferentiated public interest" into an "individual right" vindicable in the courts. The sort of scattershot redress approved today makes nonsense of our statement that the requirement of injury in fact "insures the framing of relief no broader than required by the precise facts." A claim of particularized future injury has today been made the vehicle for pursuing generalized penalties for past violations, and a threshold showing of injury in fact has become a lever that will move the world.

B

* * *

If the Court had undertaken the necessary inquiry into whether significant deterrence of the plaintiffs' feared injury was "likely," it would have had to reason something like this: Strictly speaking, no polluter is deterred by a penalty for past pollution; he is deterred by the fear of a penalty for future pollution. That fear will be virtually nonexistent if the prospective polluter knows that all emissions violators are given a free pass; it will be substantial under an emissions program such as the federal scheme here, which is regularly and notoriously enforced; it will be even higher when a prospective polluter subject to such a regularly enforced program has, as here, been the object of public charges of pollution and a suit for injunction; and it will surely be near the top of the graph when, as here, the prospective polluter has already been subjected to state penalties for the past pollution. The deterrence on which the plaintiffs must rely for standing in the present case is the marginal increase in Laidlaw's fear of future penalties that will be achieved by adding federal penalties for Laidlaw's past conduct.

I cannot say for certain that this marginal increase is zero; but I can say for certain that it is entirely speculative whether it will make the difference between these plaintiffs' suffering injury in the future and these plaintiffs' going unharmed. In fact, the assertion that it will "likely" do so is entirely farfetched. The speculativeness of that result is much greater than the speculativeness we found excessive in *Simon v. Eastern Ky. Welfare Rights Organization*, where we held that denying § 501(c)(3) charitable-deduction tax status to hospitals that refused to treat indigents was not sufficiently likely to assure future treatment of the indigent plaintiffs to support standing. And it is much greater than the speculativeness we found excessive in *Linda R.S. v. Richard D.*, where we said that "the prospect that prosecution [for nonsupport] will * * * result in payment of support can, at best, be termed only speculative."

In sum, if this case is, as the Court suggests, within the central core of "deterrence" standing, it is impossible to imagine what the "outer limits" could possibly be. The Court's expressed reluctance to define those "outer limits" serves only to disguise the fact that it has promulgated a revolutionary new doctrine of standing that will permit the entire body of public civil penalties to be handed over to enforcement by private interests.

* * *

III

Finally, I offer a few comments regarding the Court's discussion of whether FOE's claims became moot by reason of Laidlaw's substantial compliance with the permit limits. I do not disagree with the conclusion that the Court reaches. Assuming that the plaintiffs had standing to pursue civil penalties in the first instance (which they did not), their claim might well not have been mooted by Laidlaw's voluntary compliance with the permit, and leaving this fact-intensive question open for consideration on remand, as the Court does, seems sensible.[4] In reaching this disposition, however, the Court engages in a troubling discussion of the purported distinctions between the doctrines of standing and mootness. I am frankly puzzled as to why this discussion appears at all. Laidlaw's claimed compliance is squarely within the bounds of our "voluntary cessation" doctrine, which is the basis for the remand.[5] There is no reason to engage in an interesting academic excursus upon the differences between mootness and standing in order to invoke this obviously applicable rule.

* * *

By uncritically accepting vague claims of injury, the Court has turned the Article III requirement of injury in fact into a "mere pleading requirement," and by approving the novel theory that public penalties can redress anticipated private wrongs, it has come close to "mak[ing] the redressability requirement vanish." The undesirable and unconstitutional consequence of today's decision is to place the immense power of suing to enforce the public laws in private hands. I respectfully dissent.

Notes and Questions

1. a) Justice Ginsburg notes that while the DHEC action was pending, Laidlaw continued to violate its NPDES permit. Why is that relevant to the district court's inquiry? Shouldn't that be a matter of concern for the South Carolina executive branch in deciding what sort of settlement is acceptable? Has Congress made all such settlements subject to court supervision much in the manner of FED. R. CIV. P 23(e)?

b) Is it appropriate for Congress effectively to have directed the courts to deter-

---

[4] In addition to the compliance and plant-closure issues, there also remains open on remand the question whether the current suit was foreclosed because the earlier suit by the State was "diligently prosecuted." Nothing in the Court's opinion disposes of the issue. The opinion notes the District Court's finding that Laidlaw itself played a significant role in facilitating the State's action. But there is no incompatibility whatever between a defendant's facilitation of suit and the State's diligent prosecution—as prosecutions of felons who confess their crimes and turn themselves in regularly demonstrate. Laidlaw was entirely within its rights to prefer state suit to this private enforcement action; and if it had such a preference it would have been prudent—given that a State must act within 60 days of receiving notice of a citizen suit, and given the number of cases State agencies handle—for Laidlaw to make sure its case did not fall through the cracks. South Carolina's interest in the action was not a feigned last minute contrivance. It had worked with Laidlaw in resolving the problem for many years, and had previously undertaken an administrative enforcement action resulting in a consent order. South Carolina has filed an *amicus* brief arguing that allowing citizen suits to proceed despite ongoing state enforcement efforts "will provide citizens and federal judges the opportunity to relitigate and second-guess the enforcement and permitting actions of South Carolina and other States."

[5] Unlike Justice Stevens' concurrence, the opinion for the Court appears to recognize that a claim for civil penalties is moot when it is clear that no future injury to the plaintiff at the hands of the defendant can occur. The concurrence suggests that civil penalties, like traditional damages remedies, cannot be mooted by absence of threatened injury. The analogy is inapt. Traditional money damages are payable to compensate for the harm of past conduct, which subsists whether future harm is threatened or not; civil penalties are privately assessable (according to the Court) to deter threatened future harm to the plaintiff. Where there is no threat to the plaintiff, he has no claim to deterrence. The proposition that impossibility of future violation does not moot the case holds true, of course, for civil-penalty suits by the government, which do not rest upon the theory that some particular future harm is being prevented.

mine whether the government has "diligently prosecuted" an action? Should the federal courts be in the position of determining how well or poorly a litigant has prosecuted or defended an action, apart from their role in rendering a judgment? To the extent that you feel that there may be a problem with this role for the federal courts, is the problem more acute if the federal government (rather than a state government, as here) prosecutes the action?

c) Justice Scalia suggested that the idea of private attorneys general might violate Article II. Does the statute here, with its emphasis on "diligently prosecuted," inject the courts into a consideration of whether the executive has "faithfully executed" the laws, thus creating another potential constitutional problem?

2. a) What, precisely, is the injury-in-fact that plaintiffs claim to have suffered? Was Justice Scalia correct in his implication that lack of harm to the environment virtually compels the conclusion that none of the plaintiffs suffered harm even though they may have wholly subjective fears about environmental safety? The plaintiffs, of course, argued at least implicitly that Laidlaw's unlawful discharges damaged their aesthetic interest in the environment and their ability to enjoy the recreational opportunities of the North Tyger River. For many years the Court has found that cognizable as injury-in-fact. Should it, or does that give weight to Justice Scalia's charge that the Court's approach makes standing a mockery?

b) As Justice Scalia pointed out, much of the plaintiffs' injury-in-fact argument rested not on what Laidlaw's activities forced them to discontinue but rather upon what they alleged they "would" do. Should the Court have distinguished between two types of conditional statements for standing purposes, the first where the plaintiffs have been engaged in activities and "would" continue but for the defendant's conduct, and the second where the plaintiffs have never (or not for decades) engaged in such activities but allege that they "would" begin but for the defendant's conduct?

c) Is Justice Scalia's reliance on *City of Los Angeles v. Lyons* well-placed? What does the possibility of aesthetic injury-in-fact suggest?

d) Justice Scalia argues that "an initial conclusion that plaintiffs have standing is subject to reexamination, particularly if later evidence proves inconsistent with that conclusion." Does he thereby suggest that the standing inquiry remains open throughout the trial and appellate process? How far would he take that idea? Suppose a plaintiff filed a diversity action seeking to recover damages caused by the defendant's negligent driving. At the conclusion of the trial, if the jury's special verdict indicates that although the defendant drove negligently, his driving was not the proximate cause of plaintiff's injuries, should the court dismiss the action for lack of standing?

3. The Court's treatment of redressability demands consideration, not least the Court finds itself in a bind from having to defend its past decisions.

a) Justice Ginsburg notes that the Court has acknowledged the deterrent effect of civil penalties. Is that important, or is it only important that Congress intended the civil penalties to act as deterrents of future unlawful conduct? Who should evaluate the effectiveness of penalties—the legislature or the courts? If the former, then do the courts have any role at all, or could Congress effectively circumvent the injury-in-fact requirement of Article III by providing clearly nominal penalties and declaring them effective? If the latter, what standards should the courts use to determine efficacy?

b) *Linda R.S. v. Richard D.*, noted in the text on page 55, poses a problem for the Court. The majority in that case held that it was "only speculative" that the threat of criminal penalties against a parent refusing child support might cause him to commence payments. The statute in question prescribed a fixed jail term for violators. If it is too speculative to conclude that the threat of jail might be an incentive for compliance, how can the majority conclude that the threat (or imposition) of civil penalties is not too speculative as a deterrent?

The *Linda R.S.* Court argued that if the plaintiff were granted relief, the non-supporting father would be incapacitated from paying support. Isn't it nonetheless possible that the imposition of that penalty might deter future noncompliance in much the way that Justice Ginsburg's majority hypothesized that civil penalties would? Justice White dissented in *Linda R.S.*, finding the majority's reasoning "very odd." "I had always thought our civilization has assumed that the threat of penal sanctions had something more than a 'speculative effect' on a person's conduct." In other words, should Justice Ginsburg have tried so hard to live with *Linda R.S.* and its reasoning?

c) Justice Scalia argued that mere availability of civil penalties, rather than actual imposition, creates the deterrent effect. Do you think he would take the same position with respect to criminal statutes? He also argued that the sanction in the DHEC action was as great a deterrent as possible. The structure of the statute suggests that Congress felt differently. How can a court, rather than a legislature, make such a judgment?

4. Are you persuaded by the Court's treatment of *Steel Co.* (discussed in the text at page 57)? There the Court held that the plaintiffs lacked standing because the defendant had ceased its violations, but specifically noted that payment of fines to the government could not remedy the injury (failure timely to report environmental data) that the plaintiffs alleged.

> [T]he civil penalties authorized by the statute might be viewed as a sort of compensation or redress to respondent if they were payable to the respondent. But they are not. These penalties—the only damages authorized * * *—are payable to the United States Treasury. In requesting them, therefore, respondent seeks not remediation of its own injury—reimbursement for the costs it incurred as a result of the late filing—but vindication of the rule of law—the "undifferentiated public interest in the faithful execution of [the law].

Note that the *Steel Co.* Court's discussion in this respect does not turn on the timing of the action; it turns on who gets the money. Why does the deterrent value of the civil penalties suffice for redressability in *Laidlaw* but not in *Steel Co.*? In both cases, the plaintiffs surely relied upon the idea that civil penalties encourage future compliance, whether it be with respect to reporting requirements or environmentally damaging discharges. Has the majority in *Laidlaw* created a distinction without a difference?

5. a) With regard to mootness, how much voluntary cessation is enough? As the Court notes, if the defendant can show that events have eliminated any reasonable expectation of recurrence of the offending conduct, then the case is moot. "According to Laidlaw, after the Court of Appeals issued its decision but before this Court granted certiorari, the entire incinerator facility in Roebuck was permanently closed, dismantled, and put up for sale, and all discharges from the facility permanently ceased." Does that satisfy the Court's heightened cessation standard? The majority accepted FOE's argument that Laidlaw's retention of the NPDES permit might prevent a finding that there was no reasonable possibility of recurrence. How might such recurrence happen?

b) Does FOE have standing simply based on Laidlaw's permit to seek an injunction against further violations? If Laidlaw announced its intention to build another facility on the North Tyger River, would FOE be able immediately to seek an injunction against additional violations of the NPDES permit? Would it have standing? Would the case be ripe?

6. The Court suggests that mootness and standing call for different evaluations, not merely influenced by the passage of time. "[T]he prospect that a defendant will engage in (or resume) harmful conduct may be too speculative to support standing, but not too speculative to support mootness." To the extent that mootness, like standing, finds its constitutional footing in Article III, is there anything in that Article to justify the different treatment to which Justice Ginsburg adverts? If the bottom-line question is whether the plaintiff has suffered injury-in-fact and has a live controversy with the defendant, how can the Court justify what it characterizes as the "exception" to mootness of cases "capable of repetition, yet evading review"?

It may be that mootness, like standing, has both constitutional and prudential components; certainly that division seems implicit in the Court's cost-benefit analysis: "To abandon the case at an advanced stage may prove more wasteful than frugal." Does the Case-or-Controversy Clause rest on concepts of frugality?

To be added at page 139 as new Note 9:

In *Bush v. Gore*, 531 U.S. 98, 148 L.Ed. 2d 388, 121 S.Ct. 525 (2000), the United States Supreme Court essentially resolved the disputed presidential election of that year. The election depended upon which candidate received Florida's electoral votes, and the Florida popular vote was extremely close. In a suit filed by then Vice-President Al Gore, one of the candidates, the Florida Supreme Court had ordered manual recounts in all Florida counties where "undervotes," ballots that the vote scanning machines had reported as not indicating a preference for president, had not been subject to manual tabulation. After Governor George W. Bush of Texas, the other major candidate sought review, the Supreme Court reversed the Florida Supreme Court's order and remanded the case for further proceedings in a five-to-four decision. In a *per curiam* opinion the Court concluded that the Florida court's manual recount order did not meet the minimum standards required by the Equal Protection Clause. There were no uniform guidelines as to how the voters' intent was to be discerned when ballots had not been marked properly, and different counties had followed, and presumably would follow, different standards in tabulating the votes.

Justice Breyer dissented, in an opinion joined in part by Justices Stevens, Ginsburg, and Souter. He contended that the state court could have resolved the equal protection problem by imposing a uniform standard upon remand. Therefore, he did not think the Supreme Court had to act to vindicate a fundamental constitutional right. Justice Breyer went on to discuss why the majority action was not only legally wrong, but unfortunate. He noted that in characterizing political disputes that the federal courts should refrain from deciding, the Court should consider the strangeness of the issue, its intractability to judicial judgment, its momentousness, and the vulnerability of the courts as important factors, and he found that there are all present in the case. Breyer asserted that by acting in such a politicized dispute in such a divided manner, the majority risked undermining public confidence in the Court as an institution. Do you agree? If so, does that mean the Court should in no circumstances have decided the equal protection issue or that it would have been all right to decide it if it appeared that all Justices agreed?

Chapter 5

FEDERAL COMMON LAW

C. CHOOSING THE APPLICABLE LAW AND DETERMINING ITS CONTENT: FEDERAL INTERESTS OR LACK THEREOF

1. SPONTANEOUS GENERATION

To be added at page 380, immediately before "Note on Discerning the Content of State Law":

SEMTEK INTERNATIONAL INCORPORATED v. LOCKHEED MARTIN CORPORATION
Supreme Court of the United States, 2001.
531 U.S. 497, 121 S.Ct. 1021, 149 L.Ed.2d 32.

JUSTICE SCALIA delivered the opinion of the Court.

This case presents the question whether the claim-preclusive effect of a federal judgment dismissing a diversity action on statute-of-limitations grounds is determined by the law of the State in which the federal court sits.

I

Petitioner filed a complaint against respondent in California state court, alleging breach of contract and various business torts. Respondent removed the case to the United States District Court for the Central District of California on the basis of diversity of citizenship, and successfully moved to dismiss petitioner's claims as barred by California's 2-year statute of limitations. In its order of dismissal, the District Court, adopting language suggested by respondent, dismissed petitioner's claims "in [their] entirety on the merits and with prejudice." Without contesting the District Court's designation of its dismissal as "on the merits," petitioner appealed to the Court of Appeals for the Ninth Circuit, which affirmed the District Court's order. Petitioner also brought suit against respondent in the State Circuit Court for Baltimore City, Maryland, alleging the same causes of action, which were not time barred under Maryland's 3-year statute of limitations. Respondent sought injunctive relief against this action from the California federal court under the All Writs Act, 28 U.S.C. § 1651, and removed the action to the United States District Court for the District of Maryland on federal-question grounds (diversity grounds were not available because Lockheed "is a Maryland citizen." The California federal court denied the relief requested, and the Maryland federal court remanded the case to state court because the fed-

21

eral question arose only by way of defense. Following a hearing, the Maryland state court granted respondent's motion to dismiss on the ground of *res judicata*. Petitioner then returned to the California federal court and the Ninth Circuit, unsuccessfully moving both courts to amend the former's earlier order so as to indicate that the dismissal was not "on the merits." Petitioner also appealed the Maryland trial court's order of dismissal to the Maryland Court of Special Appeals. The Court of Special Appeals affirmed, holding that, regardless of whether California would have accorded claim-preclusive effect to a statute-of-limitations dismissal by one of its own courts, the dismissal by the California federal court barred the complaint filed in Maryland, since the *res judicata* effect of federal diversity judgments is prescribed by federal law, under which the earlier dismissal was on the merits and claim preclusive. After the Maryland Court of Appeals declined to review the case, we granted certiorari.

II

Petitioner contends that the outcome of this case is controlled by *Dupasseur v. Rochereau* (1875), which held that the *res judicata* effect of a federal diversity judgment "is such as would belong to judgments of the State courts rendered under similar circumstances," and may not be accorded any "higher sanctity or effect." Since, petitioner argues, the dismissal of an action on statute-of-limitations grounds by a California state court would not be claim preclusive, it follows that the similar dismissal of this diversity action by the California federal court cannot be claim preclusive. While we agree that this would be the result demanded by *Dupasseur,* the case is not dispositive because it was decided under the Conformity Act of 1872, which required federal courts to apply the procedural law of the forum State in nonequity cases. That arguably affected the outcome of the case.

Respondent, for its part, contends that the outcome of this case is controlled by Federal Rule of Civil Procedure 41(b), which provides as follows:

> Involuntary Dismissal: Effect Thereof. For failure of the plaintiff to prosecute or to comply with these rules or any order of court, a defendant may move for dismissal of an action or of any claim against the defendant. Unless the court in its order for dismissal otherwise specifies, a dismissal under this subdivision and any dismissal not provided for in this rule, other than a dismissal for lack of jurisdiction, for improper venue, or for failure to join a party under Rule 19, operates as an adjudication upon the merits.

Since the dismissal here did not "otherwise specif[y]" (indeed, it specifically stated that it *was* "on the merits"), and did not pertain to the excepted subjects of jurisdiction, venue, or joinder, it follows, respondent contends, that the dismissal "is entitled to claim preclusive effect."

Implicit in this reasoning is the unstated minor premise that all judgments denominated "on the merits" are entitled to claim-preclusive effect. That premise is not necessarily valid. The original connotation of an "on the merits" adjudication is one that actually "pass[es] directly on the substance of [a particular] claim" before the court. That connotation remains common to every jurisdiction of which we are aware. ("The prototyp[ical] [judgment on the merits is] one in which the merits of [a party's] claim are in fact adjudicated [for or] against the [party] after trial of the substantive issues"). And it is, we think, the meaning intended in those many statements to the effect that a judgment "on the merits" triggers the doctrine of *res judicata* or claim preclusion.

But over the years the meaning of the term "judgment on the merits" "has gradually undergone change," and it has come to be applied to some judgments (such as the one involved here) that do *not* pass upon the substantive merits of a claim and hence do *not* (in many jurisdictions) entail claim-preclusive effect. That is why the Restatement of Judgments has abandoned the use of the term— "because of its possibly misleading connotations."

In short, it is no longer true that a judgment "on the merits" is necessarily a judgment entitled to claim-preclusive effect; and there are a number of reasons for believing that the phrase "adjudication upon the merits" does not bear that meaning in Rule 41(b). To begin with, Rule 41(b) sets forth nothing more than a default rule for determining the import of a dismissal (a dismissal is "upon the merits," with the three stated exceptions, unless the court "otherwise specifies"). This would be a highly peculiar context in which to announce a federally prescribed rule on the complex question of claim preclusion, saying in effect, "All federal dismissals (with three specified exceptions) preclude suit elsewhere, unless the court otherwise specifies."

And even apart from the purely default character of Rule 41(b), it would be peculiar to find a rule governing the effect that must be accorded federal judgments by other courts ensconced in rules governing the internal procedures of the rendering court itself. Indeed, such a rule would arguably violate the jurisdictional limitation of the Rules Enabling Act: that the Rules "shall not abridge, enlarge or modify any substantive right." In the present case, for example, if California law left petitioner free to sue on this claim in Maryland even after the California statute of limitations had expired, the federal court's extinguishment of that right (through Rule 41(b)'s mandated claim-preclusive effect of its judgment) would seem to violate this limitation.

Moreover, as so interpreted, the Rule would in many cases violate the federalism principle of *Erie R. Co. v. Tompkins* (1938), by engendering "'substantial' variations [in outcomes] between state and federal litigation" which would "[l]ikely * * * influence the choice of a forum," *Hanna v. Plumer* (1965). With regard to the claim-preclusion issue involved in the present case, for example, the traditional rule is that expiration of the applicable statute of limitations merely bars the remedy and does not extinguish the substantive right, so that dismissal on that ground does not have claim-preclusive effect in other jurisdictions with longer, unexpired limitation periods. Out-of-state defendants sued on stale claims in California and in other States adhering to this traditional rule would systematically remove state-law suits brought against them to federal court—where, unless otherwise specified, a statute-of-limitations dismissal would bar suit everywhere.¹

Finally, if Rule 41(b) did mean what respondent suggests, we would surely have relied upon it in our cases recognizing the claim-preclusive effect of federal judgments in federal-question cases. Yet for over half a century since the promulgation of Rule 41(b), we have not once done so.

We think the key to a more reasonable interpretation of the meaning of "operates as an adjudication upon the merits" in Rule 41(b) is to be found in Rule 41(a), which, in discussing the effect of voluntary dismissal by the plaintiff, makes clear that an "adjudication upon the merits" is the opposite of a "dismissal without prejudice":

> Unless otherwise stated in the notice of dismissal or stipulation, the dismissal is without prejudice, except that a notice of dismissal operates as an adjudication upon the merits when filed by a plaintiff who has once dismissed in any court of the United States or of any state an action based on or including the same claim.

The primary meaning of "dismissal without prejudice," we think, is dismissal without barring the defendant [*sic*, probably intending "plaintiff"] from returning later, to the same court, with the same underlying claim. That will also ordinarily (though not always) have the consequence of not barring the claim from *other* courts, but its primary meaning relates to the dismissing court itself. Thus, Black's Law Dictionary defines "dismissed without prejudice" as "removed from the court's docket in such a way that the plaintiff may refile the same suit on the same claim," and defines "dismissal without prejudice" as "[a] dismissal that does not bar the plaintiff from refiling the lawsuit within the applicable limitations period."

We think, then, that the effect of the "adjudication upon the merits" default provision of Rule 41(b)—and, presumably, of the explicit order in the present case that used the language of that default provision—is simply that, unlike a dismissal "without prejudice," the dismissal in the present case barred refiling of the same claim in the United States District Court for the Central District of California. That is undoubtedly a necessary condition, but it is not a sufficient one, for claim-preclusive effect in other courts.²

---

¹ Rule 41(b), interpreted as a preclusion-establishing rule, would not have the two effects described in the preceding paragraphs—arguable violation of the Rules Enabling Act and incompatibility with *Erie R. Co. v. Tompkins* (1938)—if the court's failure to specify an other-than-on-the-merits dismissal were subject to reversal on appeal whenever it would alter the rule of claim preclusion applied by the State in which the federal court sits. No one suggests that this is the rule, and we are aware of no case that applies it.

² We do not decide whether, in a diversity case, a federal court's "dismissal upon the merits" (in the sense we have described), under circumstances where a state court would decree only a "dismissal without prejudice," abridges a "substantive right" and thus exceeds the authorization of the Rules Enabling Act. We think the situation will present itself more rarely than would the arguable violation of the Act that would ensue from interpreting Rule 41(b) as a rule of claim preclusion; and if it is a violation, can be more easily dealt with on direct appeal.

III

Having concluded that the claim-preclusive effect, in Maryland, of this California federal diversity judgment is dictated neither by *Dupasseur v. Rochereau,* as petitioner contends, nor by Rule 41(b), as respondent contends, we turn to consideration of what determines the issue. Neither the Full Faith and Credit Clause nor the full faith and credit statute addresses the question. By their terms they govern the effects to be given only to state-court judgments (and, in the case of the statute, to judgments by courts of territories and possessions). And no other federal textual provision, neither of the Constitution nor of any statute, addresses the claim-preclusive effect of a judgment in a federal diversity action.

It is also true, however, that no federal textual provision addresses the claim-preclusive effect of a federal-court judgment in a federal-question case, yet we have long held that States cannot give those judgments merely whatever effect they would give their own judgments, but must accord them the effect that this Court prescribes. The reasoning of that line of cases suggests, moreover, that even when States are allowed to give federal judgments (notably, judgments in diversity cases) no more than the effect accorded to state judgments, that disposition is by direction of *this* Court, which has the last word on the claim-preclusive effect of *all* federal judgments:

> It is true that for some purposes and within certain limits it is only required that the judgments of the courts of the United States shall be given the same force and effect as are given the judgments of the courts of the States wherein they are rendered; but it is equally true that whether a Federal judgment has been given due force and effect in the state court is a Federal question reviewable by this court, which will determine for itself whether such judgment has been given due weight or otherwise. * * *
>
> When is the state court obliged to give to Federal judgments only the force and effect it gives to state court judgments within its own jurisdiction? Such cases are distinctly pointed out in the opinion of Mr. Justice Bradley in *Dupasseur v. Rochereau* [which stated that the case was a diversity case, applying state law under state procedure]."

In other words, in *Dupasseur* the State was allowed (indeed, required) to give a federal diversity judgment no more effect than it would accord one of its own judgments only because reference to state law was *the federal rule that this Court deemed appropriate*. In short, federal common law governs the claim-preclusive effect of a dismissal by a federal court sitting in diversity.

It is left to us, then, to determine the appropriate federal rule. And despite the sea change that has occurred in the background law since *Dupasseur* was decided—not only repeal of the Conformity Act but also the watershed decision of this Court in *Erie*—we think the result decreed by *Dupasseur* continues to be correct for diversity cases. Since state, rather than federal, substantive law is at issue there is no need for a uniform federal rule. And indeed, nationwide uniformity in the substance of the matter is better served by having the same claim-preclusive rule (the state rule) apply whether the dismissal has been ordered by a state or a federal court. This is, it seems to us, a classic case for adopting, as the federally prescribed rule of decision, the law that would be applied by state courts in the State in which the federal diversity court sits. As we have alluded to above, any other rule would produce the sort of "forum-shopping * * * and * * * inequitable administration of the laws" that *Erie* seeks to avoid, since filing in, or removing to, federal court would be encouraged by the divergent effects that the litigants would anticipate from likely grounds of dismissal.

This federal reference to state law will not obtain, of course, in situations in which the state law is incompatible with federal interests. If, for example, state law did not accord claim-preclusive effect to dismissals for willful violation of discovery orders, federal courts' interest in the integrity of their own processes might justify a contrary federal rule. No such conflict with potential federal interests exists in the present case. Dismissal of this state cause of action was decreed by the California federal court only because the California statute of limitations so required; and there is no conceivable federal interest in giving that time bar more effect in other courts than the California courts themselves would impose.

* * *

Because the claim-preclusive effect of the California federal court's dismissal "upon the merits" of petitioner's action on statute-of-limitations grounds is governed by a federal rule that in turn incorporates California's law of claim preclusion (the content of which we do not pass upon today), the Maryland Court of Special Appeals erred in holding that the dismissal necessarily precluded the bringing of this action in the Maryland courts. The judgment is reversed, and the case remanded for further proceedings not inconsistent with this opinion.

It is so ordered.

Notes and Questions

1. The Court notes *Dupasseur* as an example of a state giving a federal judgment the same effect as a state judgment, not more, because of the Court's own direction. Is this incompatible with Justice Scalia's opening mention that the Court decided *Dupasseur* pursuant to the Conformity Act of 1872, which prescribed federal courts' use of state procedure? In other words, was it the Court's direction or Congress's that produced the result?

2. Is the Court's adoption of state law as the content of the federal common law rule at odds with its previous insistence in *Boyle* (authored by Justice Scalia) and *Atherton* that the Court should not make federal common law unless it first finds what Justice Scalia called "a significant conflict" between state law and federal interests? If so, should one conclude that the Court has shifted its course on federal common law? If not, how can one reconcile the approach in *Semtek* with that of *Boyle* and *Atherton*? The latter seemed to say that state law remained in place unless some conflict with federal interests required its displacement. What is the conflict here, or indeed, in any case in which the Court directs adoption of state law as the content of federal common law?

3. IMPLYING PRIVATE RIGHTS OF ACTION

To be added at page 443, after Note 8:

ALEXANDER v. SANDOVAL
Supreme Court of the United States, 2001.
___ U.S. ___, 121 S.Ct. 1511, 149 L.Ed.2d 517.

JUSTICE SCALIA delivered the opinion of the Court.

This case presents the question whether private individuals may sue to enforce disparate-impact regulations promulgated under Title VI of the Civil Rights Act of 1964.

I

The Alabama Department of Public Safety (Department), of which petitioner James Alexander is the Director, accepted grants of financial assistance from the United States Department of Justice (DOJ) and Department of Transportation (DOT) and so subjected itself to the restrictions of Title VI of the Civil Rights Act of 1964. Section 601 of that Title provides that no person shall, "on the ground of race, color, or national origin, be excluded from participation in, be denied the benefits of, or be subjected to discrimination under any program or activity" covered by Title VI. Section 602 authorizes federal agencies "to effectuate the provisions of [§ 601] * * * by issuing rules, regulations, or orders of general applicability," and the DOJ in an exercise of this authority promulgated a regulation forbidding funding recipients to "utilize criteria or methods of administration which have the effect of subjecting individuals to discrimination because of their race, color, or national origin * * *."

The State of Alabama amended its Constitution in 1990 to declare English "the official language of the state of Alabama." Pursuant to this provision and, petitioners have argued, to advance public safety, the Department decided to administer state driver's license examinations only in English. Respondent Sandoval, as representative of a class, brought suit in the United States District Court for the Middle District of Alabama to enjoin the English-only policy, arguing that it violated the DOJ regulation because it had the effect of subjecting non-English speakers to discrimination based on their national origin. The District Court agreed. It enjoined the policy and ordered the Department to accommodate non-English speakers. Petitioners appealed to the Court of Appeals for the Eleventh Circuit, which affirmed. Both courts rejected petitioners' argument that Title VI did not provide respondents a cause of action to enforce the regulation.

We do not inquire here whether the DOJ regulation was authorized by § 602, or whether the courts below were correct to hold that the English-only policy had the effect of discriminating on the basis of national origin. The petition for writ of certiorari raised, and we agreed to review, only the question posed in the first paragraph of this opinion: whether there is a private cause of action to enforce the regulation.

II

Although Title VI has often come to this Court, it is fair to say (indeed, perhaps an understatement) that our opinions have not eliminated all uncertainty regarding its commands. For purposes of the present case, however, it is clear from our decisions, from Congress's amendments of Title VI, and from the parties' concessions that three aspects of Title VI must be taken as given. First, private individuals may sue to enforce § 601 of Title VI and obtain both injunctive relief and damages. In *Cannon v. University of Chicago* (1979) the Court held that a private right of action existed to enforce Title IX of the Education Amendments of 1972. The reasoning of that decision embraced the existence of a private right to enforce Title VI as well. * * * Congress has since ratified *Cannon*'s holding. Section 1003 of the Rehabilitation Act Amendments of 1986 expressly abrogated States' sovereign immunity against suits brought in federal court to enforce Title VI and provided that in a suit against a State "remedies (including remedies both at law and in equity) are available * * * to the same extent as such remedies are available * * * in the suit against any public or private entity other than a State." We recognized in *Franklin v. Gwinnett County Public Schools* (1992), that § 2000d-7 "cannot be read except as a validation of *Cannon*'s holding." It is thus beyond dispute that private individuals may sue to enforce § 601.

Second, it is similarly beyond dispute—and no party disagrees—that § 601 prohibits only intentional discrimination. In *Regents of Univ. of Cal. v. Bakke* (1978), the Court reviewed a decision of the California Supreme Court that had enjoined the University of California Medical School from "according any consideration to race in its admissions process." Essential to the Court's holding reversing that aspect of the California court's decision was the determination that § 601 "proscribe[s] only those racial classifications that would violate the Equal Protection Clause or the Fifth Amendment." In *Guardians Assn. v. Civil Serv. Comm'n of New York City* (1983), the Court made clear that under *Bakke* only intentional discrimination was forbidden by § 601. (Powell, J., joined by Burger, C.J., and Rehnquist, J., concurring in judgment); (O'Connor, J., concurring in judgment); (Stevens, J., joined by Brennan and Blackmun, JJ., dissenting). What we said in *Alexander v. Choate* (1985) is true today: "Title VI itself directly reach[es] only instances of intentional discrimination."[3]

Third, we must assume for purposes of deciding this case that regulations promulgated under § 602 of Title VI may validly proscribe activities that have a disparate impact on racial groups, even though such activities are permissible under § 601. Though no opinion of this Court has held that, five Justices in *Guardians* voiced that view of the law at least as alternative grounds for their decisions, and dictum in *Alexander v. Choate* is to the same effect. These statements are in considerable tension with the rule of *Bakke* and *Guardians* that § 601 forbids only intentional discrimination, but petitioners have not challenged the regulations here. We therefore assume for the purposes of deciding this case

---

[3] Since the parties do not dispute this point, it is puzzling to see Justice Stevens go out of his way to disparage the decisions in *Regents of Univ. of Cal. v. Bakke* and *Guardians Assn. v. Civil Serv. Comm'n of New York City* as "somewhat haphazard," particularly since he had already accorded *stare decisis* effect to the former 18 years ago and since he participated in creating the latter. * * *

that the DOJ and DOT regulations proscribing activities that have a disparate impact on the basis of race are valid.

Respondents assert that the issue in this case, like the first two described above, has been resolved by our cases. To reject a private cause of action to enforce the disparate-impact regulations, they say, we would "[have] to ignore the actual language of *Guardians* and *Cannon*." The language in *Cannon* to which respondents refer does not in fact support their position, as we shall discuss * * *. But in any event, this Court is bound by holdings, not language. *Cannon* was decided on the assumption that the University of Chicago had intentionally discriminated against petitioner (noting that respondents "admitted *arguendo*" that petitioner's "application for admission to medical school was denied by the respondents because she is a woman"). It therefore *held* that Title IX created a private right of action to enforce its ban on intentional discrimination, but had no occasion to consider whether the right reached regulations barring disparate-impact discrimination.[4] In *Guardians*, the Court *held* that private individuals could not recover compensatory damages under Title VI except for intentional discrimination. Five Justices in addition voted to uphold the disparate-impact regulations (four would have declared them invalid), but of those five, three expressly reserved the question of a direct private right of action to enforce the regulations, saying that "[w]hether a cause of action against private parties exists directly under the regulations * * * [is a] questio[n] that [is] not presented by this case." (Stevens, J., dissenting).[5] Thus, only two Justices had cause to reach the issue that respondents say the "actual language" of *Guardians* resolves. Neither that case[6] nor any other in this Court, has held that the private right of action exists.

---

[4] Although the dissent acknowledges that "the breadth of [*Cannon*'s] precedent is a matter upon which reasonable jurists may differ," it disagrees with our reading of *Cannon*'s holding because it thinks the distinction we draw between disparate-impact and intentional discrimination was "wholly foreign" to that opinion. *Cannon*, however, was decided less than one year after the Court in *Bakke* had drawn precisely that distinction *with respect to Title VI*, and it is absurd to think that *Cannon* meant, without discussion, to ban under Title IX the very disparate-impact discrimination that *Bakke* said Title VI permitted. The *only* discussion in *Cannon* of Title IX's scope is found in Justice Powell's dissenting opinion, which simply assumed that the conclusion that Title IX would be limited to intentional discrimination was "forgone in light of our holding" in *Bakke*. The dissent's additional claim that *Cannon* provided a private right of action for "all the discrimination prohibited by the *regulatory scheme* contained in Title IX" (emphasis added), simply begs the question at the heart of this case, which is whether a right of action to enforce disparate-impact regulations must be independently identified.

[5] We of course accept the statement by the author of the dissent that he "thought" at the time of *Guardians* that disparate-impact regulations could be enforced "in an implied action against private parties." But we have the better interpretation of what our colleague wrote in *Guardians*. In the closing section of his opinion, Justice Stevens concluded that because respondents in that case had "violated the petitioners' rights under [the] regulations * * * [t]he petitioners were therefore entitled to the compensation they sought under 42 U.S.C. § 1983 and were awarded by the District Court." The passage omits any mention of a direct private right of action to enforce the regulations, and the footnote we have quoted in text—which appears immediately after this concluding sentence—makes clear that the omission was not accidental.

[6] Ultimately, the dissent agrees that "the holding in *Guardians* does not compel the conclusion that a private right of action exists to enforce the Title VI regulations against private parties."

Nor does it follow straightaway from the three points we have taken as given that Congress must have intended a private right of action to enforce disparate-impact regulations. We do not doubt that regulations applying § 601's ban on intentional discrimination are covered by the cause of action to enforce that section. Such regulations, if valid and reasonable, authoritatively construe the statute itself, and it is therefore meaningless to talk about a separate cause of action to enforce the regulations apart from the statute. A Congress that intends the statute to be enforced through a private cause of action intends the authoritative interpretation of the statute to be so enforced as well. The many cases that respondents say have "assumed" that a cause of action to enforce a statute includes one to enforce its regulations illustrate (to the extent that cases in which an issue was not presented can illustrate anything) only this point; each involved regulations of the type we have just described, as respondents conceded at oral argument. Our decision in *Lau v. Nichols* (1974) falls within the same category. The Title VI regulations at issue in *Lau*, similar to the ones at issue here, forbade funding recipients to take actions which had the effect of discriminating on the basis of race, color, or national origin. Unlike our later cases, however, the Court in *Lau* interpreted § 601 itself to proscribe disparate-impact discrimination, saying that it "rel[ied] solely on § 601 * * * to reverse the Court of Appeals," and that the disparate-impact regulations simply "[made] sure that recipients of federal aid * * * conduct[ed] any federally financed projects consistently with § 601."[7]

We must face now the question avoided by *Lau*, because we have since rejected *Lau*'s interpretation of § 601 as reaching beyond intentional discrimination. It is clear now that the disparate-impact regulations do not simply apply § 601—since they indeed forbid conduct that § 601 permits—and therefore clear that the private right of action to enforce § 601 does not include a private right to enforce these regulations. That right must come, if at all, from the independent force of § 602. As stated earlier, we assume for purposes of this decision that § 602 confers the authority to promulgate disparate-impact regulations;[8] the question remains whether it confers a private right of action to enforce them. If not, we must conclude that a failure to comply with regulations promulgated under § 602 that is not also a failure to comply with § 601 is not actionable.

Implicit in our discussion thus far has been a particular understanding of the genesis of private causes of action. Like substantive federal law itself, private rights of action to enforce federal law must be created by Congress. The

---

[7] It is true, as the dissent points out, that three Justices who concurred in the result in *Lau* relied on regulations promulgated under § 602 to support their position. But the five Justices who made up the majority did not, and their holding is not made coextensive with the concurrence because their opinion does not expressly preclude (is "consistent with") the concurrence's approach. The Court would be in an odd predicament if a concurring minority of the Justices could force the majority to address a point they found it unnecessary (and did not wish) to address, under compulsion of Justice Stevens' new principle that silence implies agreement.

[8] For this reason, the dissent's extended discussion of the scope of agencies' regulatory authority under § 602, is beside the point. We cannot help observing, however, how strange it is to say that disparate-impact regulations are "inspired by, at the service of, and inseparably intertwined with" § 601 when § 601 permits the very behavior that the regulations forbid.

judicial task is to interpret the statute Congress has passed to determine whether it displays an intent to create not just a private right but also a private remedy. Statutory intent on this latter point is determinative. Without it, a cause of action does not exist and courts may not create one, no matter how desirable that might be as a policy matter, or how compatible with the statute. "Raising up causes of action where a statute has not created them may be a proper function for common-law courts, but not for federal tribunals." *Lampf, Pleva, Lipkind, Prupis & Petigrow v. Gilbertson* (1991) (Scalia, J., concurring in part and concurring in judgment).

Respondents would have us revert in this case to the understanding of private causes of action that held sway 40 years ago when Title VI was enacted. That understanding is captured by the Court's statement in *J.I. Case Co. v. Borak* (1964), that "it is the duty of the courts to be alert to provide such remedies as are necessary to make effective the congressional purpose" expressed by a statute. We abandoned that understanding in *Cort v. Ash* (1975)—which itself interpreted a statute enacted under the *ancien regime*—and have not returned to it since. Not even when interpreting the same Securities Exchange Act of 1934 that was at issue in *Borak* have we applied *Borak*'s method for discerning and defining causes of action. Having sworn off the habit of venturing beyond Congress's intent, we will not accept respondents' invitation to have one last drink.

Nor do we agree with the Government that our cases interpreting statutes enacted prior to *Cort v. Ash* have given "dispositive weight" to the "expectations" that the enacting Congress had formed "in light of the 'contemporary legal context.'" Only three of our legion implied-right-of-action cases have found this sort of "contemporary legal context" relevant, and two of those involved Congress's enactment (or reenactment) of the verbatim statutory text that courts had previously interpreted to create a private right of action. In the third case, this sort of "contemporary legal context" simply buttressed a conclusion independently supported by the text of the statute. We have never accorded dispositive weight to context shorn of text. In determining whether statutes create private rights of action, as in interpreting statutes generally, legal context matters only to the extent it clarifies text.

We therefore begin (and find that we can end) our search for Congress's intent with the text and structure of Title VI. Section 602 authorizes federal agencies "to effectuate the provisions of [§ 601] * * * by issuing rules, regulations, or orders of general applicability." It is immediately clear that the "rights-creating" language so critical to the Court's analysis in *Cannon* of § 601 is completely absent from § 602. Whereas § 601 decrees that "[n]o person * * * shall * * * be subjected to discrimination," the text of § 602 provides that "[e]ach Federal department and agency * * * is authorized and directed to effectuate the provisions of [§ 601]." Far from displaying congressional intent to create new rights, § 602 limits agencies to "effectuat[ing]" rights already created by § 601. And the focus of § 602 is twice removed from the individuals who will ultimately benefit from Title VI's protection. Statutes that focus on the person regulated rather than the individuals protected create "no implication of an intent to confer rights on a particular class of persons." *California v. Sierra Club* (1981). Section 602 is yet a step further removed: it focuses neither on the individuals protected nor even on the funding recipients being regulated, but on the agencies that will do the regulating. Like the statute found not to create a right of action in *Universities Research Assn., Inc. v. Coutu* (1981), § 602 is "phrased as a directive to federal agencies engaged in the distribution of public funds." When this is true, "[t]here [is] far less reason to infer a private remedy in favor of individual persons." [*Cannon v. University of Chicago* (1979).] So far as we can tell, this authorizing portion of § 602 reveals no congressional intent to create a private right of action.

Nor do the methods that § 602 goes on to provide for enforcing its authorized regulations manifest an intent to create a private remedy; if anything, they suggest the opposite. Section 602 empowers agencies to enforce their regulations either by terminating funding to the "particular program, or part thereof," that has violated the regulation or "by any other means authorized by law." No enforcement action may be taken, however, "until the department or agency concerned has advised the appropriate person or persons of the failure to comply with the requirement and has determined that compliance cannot be secured by voluntary means." And every agency enforcement action is subject to judicial review. If an agency attempts to terminate program funding, still more restrictions apply. The agency head must "file with the committees of the House and Senate having legislative jurisdiction over the program or activity involved a full written report of the circumstances and the grounds for such action." And the termination of funding does not "become effective until thirty days have elapsed after the filing of such report." Whatever these elaborate restrictions on agency enforcement may imply for the private enforcement of rights created *outside* of § 602, they tend to contradict a congressional intent to create privately enforceable rights through § 602 itself. The express provision of one method of enforcing a substantive rule suggests that Congress intended to preclude others. Sometimes the suggestion is so strong that it precludes a finding of congressional intent to create a private right of action, even though other aspects of the statute (such as language making the would-be plaintiff "a member of the class for whose benefit the statute was enacted") suggest the contrary. And as our § 1983 cases show, some remedial schemes foreclose a private cause of action to enforce even those statutes that admittedly create substantive private rights. In the present case, the claim of exclusivity for the express remedial scheme does not even have to overcome such obstacles. The question whether § 602's remedial scheme can overbear other evidence of congressional intent is simply not presented, since we have found no evidence anywhere in the text to suggest that Congress intended to create a private right to enforce regulations promulgated under § 602.

Both the Government and respondents argue that the *regulations* contain rights-creating language and so must be privately enforceable, but that argument skips an analytical step. Language in a regulation may invoke a private right of action that Congress through statutory text created, but it may not create a right that Congress has not. Thus, when a statute has provided a general authorization for private enforcement of regulations, it may perhaps be correct that the intent displayed in each regulation can determine whether or not it is privately enforceable. But it is most certainly incorrect to say that language in a regulation can conjure up a private cause of action that has not been authorized by Congress.

Agencies may play the sorcerer's apprentice but not the sorcerer himself.

The last string to respondents' and the Government's bow is their argument that two amendments to Title VI "ratified" this Court's decisions finding an implied private right of action to enforce the disparate-impact regulations. One problem with this argument is that, as explained above, none of our decisions establishes (or even assumes) the private right of action at issue here, which is why in *Guardians* three Justices were able expressly to reserve the question. Incorporating our cases in the amendments would thus not help respondents. Another problem is that the incorporation claim itself is flawed. Section 1003 of the Rehabilitation Act Amendments of 1986, on which only respondents rely, by its terms applies only to suits "for a violation of a *statute*." ([E]mphasis added). It therefore does not speak to suits for violations of regulations that go beyond the statutory proscription of § 601. Section 6 of the Civil Rights Restoration Act of 1987 is even less on point. That provision amends Title VI to make the term "program or activity" cover larger portions of the institutions receiving federal financial aid than it had previously covered. It is impossible to understand what this has to do with implied causes of action—which is why we declared * * * that § 6 did not "in any way alte[r] the existing rights of action and the corresponding remedies permissible under * * * Title VI." Respondents point to *Merrill Lynch, Pierce, Fenner & Smith, Inc. v. Curran* [(1982)], which inferred congressional intent to ratify lower court decisions regarding a particular statutory provision when Congress comprehensively revised the statutory scheme but did not amend that provision. But we recently criticized *Curran*'s reliance on congressional inaction, saying that "[a]s a general matter * * * [the] argumen[t] deserve[s] little weight in the interpretive process." And when, as here, Congress has not comprehensively revised a statutory scheme but has made only isolated amendments, we have spoken more bluntly: "It is 'impossible to assert with any degree of assurance that congressional failure to act represents' affirmative congressional approval of the Court's statutory interpretation."

Neither as originally enacted nor as later amended does Title VI display an intent to create a freestanding private right of action to enforce regulations promulgated under § 602.[8] We therefore hold that no such right of action exists. * * *

The judgment of the Court of Appeals is reversed.

It is so ordered.

---

[8] The dissent complains that we "offe[r] little affirmative support" for this conclusion. But as Justice Stevens has previously recognized in an opinion for the Court, "affirmative" evidence of congressional intent must be provided for an implied remedy, not against it, for without such intent "the essential predicate for implication of a private remedy simply does not exist." The dissent's assertion that "petitioners *have* marshaled substantial affirmative evidence that a private right of action exists to enforce Title VI *and the regulations validly promulgated thereunder*" (second emphasis added) once again begs the question whether authorization of a private right of action to enforce a statute constitutes authorization of a private right of action to enforce regulations that go beyond what the statute itself requires.

JUSTICE STEVENS, with whom JUSTICE SOUTER, JUSTICE GINSBURG, and JUSTICE BREYER join, dissenting.

In 1964, as part of a groundbreaking and comprehensive civil rights Act, Congress prohibited recipients of federal funds from discriminating on the basis of race, ethnicity, or national origin. Pursuant to powers expressly delegated by that Act, the federal agencies and departments responsible for awarding and administering federal contracts immediately adopted regulations prohibiting federal contractees from adopting policies that have the "effect" of discriminating on those bases. At the time of the promulgation of these regulations, prevailing principles of statutory construction assumed that Congress intended a private right of action whenever such a cause of action was necessary to protect individual rights granted by valid federal law. Relying both on this presumption and on independent analysis of Title VI, this Court has repeatedly and consistently affirmed the right of private individuals to bring civil suits to enforce rights guaranteed by Title VI. A fair reading of those cases, and coherent implementation of the statutory scheme, requires the same result under Title VI's implementing regulations.

In separate lawsuits spanning several decades, we have endorsed an action identical in substance to the one brought in this case, demonstrated that Congress intended a private right of action to protect the rights guaranteed by Title VI, and concluded that private individuals may seek declaratory and injunctive relief against state officials for violations of regulations promulgated pursuant to Title VI. Giving fair import to our language and our holdings, every Court of Appeals to address the question has concluded that a private right of action exists to enforce the rights guaranteed both by the text of Title VI and by any regulations validly promulgated pursuant to that Title, and Congress has adopted several statutes that appear to ratify the status quo.

Today, in a decision unfounded in our precedent and hostile to decades of settled expectations, a majority of this Court carves out an important exception to the right of private action long recognized under Title VI. In so doing, the Court makes three distinct, albeit interrelated, errors. First, the Court provides a muddled account of both the reasoning and the breadth of our prior decisions endorsing a private right of action under Title VI, thereby obscuring the conflict between those opinions and today's decision. Second, the Court offers a flawed and unconvincing analysis of the relationship between §§ 601 and 602 of the Civil Rights Act of 1964, ignoring more plausible and persuasive explanations detailed in our prior opinions. Finally, the Court badly misconstrues the theoretical linchpin of our decision in *Cannon v. University of Chicago*, mistaking that decision's careful contextual analysis for judicial fiat.

I

The majority is undoubtedly correct that this Court has never said in so many words that a private right of action exists to enforce the disparate-impact regulations promulgated under § 602. However, the failure of our cases to state this conclusion explicitly does not absolve the Court of the responsibility to canvass our prior opinions for guidance. Reviewing these opinions with the care they deserve, I reach the same conclusion as the Courts of Appeals: This Court has already considered the question presented today and concluded that a private right of action exists.[1]

When this Court faced an identical case 27 years ago, all the Justices believed that private parties could bring lawsuits under Title VI and its implementing regulations to enjoin the provision of governmental services in a manner that discriminated against non-English speakers. *See Lau v. Nichols* (1974). While five Justices saw no need to go beyond the command of § 601, Chief Justice Burger, Justice Stewart, and Justice Blackmun relied specifically and exclusively on the regulations to support the private action. There is nothing in the majority's opinion in *Lau*, or in earlier opinions of the Court, that is not fully consistent with the analysis of the concurring Justices or that would have differentiated between private actions to enforce the text of § 601 and private actions to enforce the regulations promulgated pursuant to § 602. *See Guardians* (principal opinion of White, J.) (describing this history and noting that, up to that point, no Justice had ever expressed disagreement with Justice Stewart's analysis in *Lau*).[2]

Five years later, we more explicitly considered whether a private right of action exists to enforce the guarantees of Title VI and its gender-based twin, Title IX. In [*Cannon v. University of Chicago*], we examined the text of the statutes, analyzed the purpose of the laws, and canvassed the relevant legislative history. Our conclusion was unequivocal: "We have no doubt that Congress intended to create Title IX remedies comparable to those available under Title VI and that it understood Title VI as authorizing an implied private cause of action for victims of the prohibited discrimination."

The majority acknowledges that *Cannon* is binding precedent with regard to both Title VI and Title IX, but seeks to limit the scope of its holding to cases involving allegations of intentional discrimination. The distinction the majority attempts to impose is wholly foreign to *Cannon*'s text and reasoning. The opinion in *Cannon* consistently treats the question presented in that case as whether a private right of action exists to enforce "Title IX" (and by extension "Title VI"), and does not draw any distinctions between the various types of discrimination outlawed by the operation of those statutes. Though the opinion did not reach out to affirmatively preclude the drawing of every conceivable distinction, it could hardly have been more clear as to the scope of its holding: A private right of action exists for "victims of *the* prohibited discrimination." ([E]mphasis added.) Not some of the prohibited discrimination, but all of it.[4]

---

[1] Just about every Court of Appeals has either explicitly or implicitly held that a private right of action exists to enforce all of the regulations issued pursuant to Title VI, including the disparate-impact regulations. No Court of Appeals has ever reached a contrary conclusion. [Justice Stevens noted that the Second Circuit suggested in 2000 that the question might be open.]

[2] Indeed, it would have been remarkable if the majority had offered any disagreement with the concurring analysis as the concurring Justices grounded their argument in well-established principles for determining the availability of remedies under regulations, principles that all but one Member of the Court had endorsed the previous Term. The other decision the concurring Justices cited for this well-established principle was unanimous and only five years old.

[4] The majority is undoubtedly correct that *Cannon* was not a case about the substance of Title IX but rather about the remedies available under that statute. Therefore, *Cannon* can not stand

Moreover, *Cannon* was itself a disparate-impact case. In that case, the plaintiff brought suit against two private universities challenging medical school admissions policies that set age limits for applicants. Plaintiff, a 39-year-old woman, alleged that these rules had the effect of discriminating against women because the incidence of interrupted higher education is higher among women than among men. In providing a shorthand description of her claim in the text of the opinion, we ambiguously stated that she had alleged that she was denied admission "because she is a woman," but we appended a lengthy footnote setting forth the details of her disparate-impact claim. Other than the shorthand description of her claim, there is not a word in the text of the opinion even suggesting that she had made the improbable allegation that the University of Chicago and Northwestern University had intentionally discriminated against women. In the context of the entire opinion (including both its analysis and its uncontested description of the facts of the case), that single ambiguous phrase provides no basis for limiting the case's holding to incidents of intentional discrimination. If anything, the fact that the phrase "because she is a woman" encompasses both intentional and disparate-impact claims should have made it clear that the reasoning in the opinion was equally applicable to both types of claims. In any event, the *holding* of the case certainly applied to the disparate-impact claim that was described in detail in footnote 1 of the opinion.

* * *

In summary, there is clear precedent of this Court for the proposition that the plaintiffs in this case can seek injunctive relief either through an implied right of action or through § 1983. Though the holding in *Guardians* does not compel the conclusion that a private right of action exists to enforce the Title VI regulations against private parties, the rationales of the relevant opinions strongly imply that result. When that fact is coupled with our holding in *Cannon* and our unanimous decision in *Lau*, the answer to the question presented in this case is overdetermined. Even absent my continued belief that Congress intended a private right of action to enforce both Title VI and its implementing regulations, I would answer the question presented in the affirmative and affirm the decision of the Court of Appeals as a matter of *stare decisis*.[9]

---

as a precedent for the proposition either that Title IX and its implementing regulations reach intentional discrimination or that they do not do so. What *Cannon* did hold is that all the discrimination prohibited by the regulatory scheme contained in Title IX may be the subject of a private lawsuit. As the Court today concedes that *Cannon*'s holding applies to Title VI claims as well as Title IX claims and assumes that the regulations promulgated pursuant to § 602 are validly promulgated antidiscrimination measures, it is clear that today's opinion is in substantial tension with *Cannon*'s reasoning and holding.

[9] The settled expectations the Court undercuts today derive not only from judicial decisions, but also from the consistent statements and actions of Congress. Congress' actions over the last two decades reflect a clear understanding of the existence of a private right action to enforce Title VI and its implementing regulations. In addition to numerous other small-scale amendments, Congress has twice adopted legislation expanding the reach of Title VI. Both of these bills were adopted after this Court's decision in *Lau, Cannon,* and *Guardians,* and after most of the Courts of Appeals had affirmatively acknowledged an implied private right of action to enforce the disparate impact regulations. Their legislative histories explicitly reflect the fact that both proponents and opponents of the bills assumed that the full breadth of Title VI (including the disparate impact regu-

II

Underlying the majority's dismissive treatment of our prior cases is a flawed understanding of the structure of Title VI and, more particularly, of the relationship between §§ 601 and 602. To some extent, confusion as to the relationship between the provisions is understandable, as Title VI is a deceptively simple statute. * * *

On the surface, the relationship between §§ 601 and 602 is unproblematic—§ 601 states a basic principle, § 602 authorizes agencies to develop detailed plans for defining the contours of the principle and ensuring its enforcement. In the context of federal civil rights law, however, nothing is ever so simple. As actions to enforce § 601's antidiscrimination principle have worked their way through the courts, we have developed a body of law giving content to § 601's broadly worded commitment. As the majority emphasizes today, the Judiciary's understanding of what conduct may be remedied in actions brought directly under § 601 is, in certain ways, more circumscribed than the conduct prohibited by the regulations.

Given that seeming peculiarity, it is necessary to examine closely the relationship between §§ 601 and 602, in order to understand the purpose and import of the regulations at issue in this case. For the most part, however, the majority ignores this task, assuming that the judicial decisions interpreting § 601 provide an authoritative interpretation of its true meaning and treating the regulations promulgated by the agencies charged with administering the statute as poor step-cousins—either parroting the text of § 601 (in the case of regulations that prohibit intentional discrimination) or forwarding an agenda untethered to § 601's mandate (in the case of disparate-impact regulations).

* * * Section 602 exists for the sole purpose of forwarding the antidiscrimination ideals laid out in § 601. The majority's persistent belief that the two sections somehow forward different agendas finds no support in the statute. Nor does Title VI anywhere suggest, let alone state, that for the purpose of determining their legal effect, the "rules, regulations, [and] orders of general applicability" adopted by the agencies are to be bifurcated by the judiciary into two categories based on how closely the courts believe the regulations track the text of § 601.

* * * For three decades, we have treated § 602 as granting the responsible agencies the power to issue broad prophylactic rules aimed at realizing the vision laid out in § 601, even if the conduct captured by these rules is at times broader than that which would otherwise be prohibited.

In *Lau*, our first Title VI case, the only three Justices whose understanding of § 601 required them to reach the question explicitly endorsed the power of the agencies to adopt broad prophylactic rules to enforce the aims of the statute. As Justice Stewart explained, regulations promulgated pursuant to § 602 may "go

---

lations promulgated pursuant to it) would be enforceable in private actions. * * * Thus, this case goes well beyond the normal situation in which "after a comprehensive reexamination and significant amendment" Congress "left intact the statutory provisions under which the federal courts had implied a private cause of action." Here, there is no need to rest on presumptions of knowledge and ratification, because the direct evidence of Congress' understanding is plentiful.

beyond * * * § 601" as long as they are "reasonably related" to its antidiscrimination mandate. In *Guardians*, at least three Members of the Court adopted a similar understanding of the statute. Finally, just 16 years ago, our unanimous opinion in *Alexander v. Choate* (1985), treated this understanding of Title VI's structure as settled law. Writing for the Court, Justice Marshall aptly explained the interpretation of § 602's grant of regulatory power that necessarily underlies our prior caselaw: "In essence, then, we [have] held that Title VI [has] delegated to the agencies in the first instance the complex determination of what sorts of disparate impacts upon minorities constituted sufficiently significant social problems, and [are] readily enough remediable, to warrant altering the practices of the federal grantees that ha[ve] produced those impacts."

* * *

The "effects" regulations at issue in this case represent the considered judgment of the relevant agencies that discrimination on the basis of race, ethnicity, and national origin by federal contractees are significant social problems that might be remedied, or at least ameliorated, by the application of a broad prophylactic rule. Given the judgment underlying them, the regulations are inspired by, at the service of, and inseparably intertwined with § 601's antidiscrimination mandate. Contrary to the majority's suggestion, they "appl[y]" § 601's prohibition on discrimination just as surely as the intentional discrimination regulations the majority concedes are privately enforceable.

* * *

Our conclusion that the legislation only encompasses intentional discrimination was never the subject of thorough consideration by a Court focused on that question. In *Bakke*, five Members of this Court concluded that § 601 only prohibits race-based affirmative action programs in situations where the Equal Protection Clause would impose a similar ban.[15] In *Guardians*, the majority of the Court held that the analysis of those five Justices in *Bakke* compelled *as a matter of stare decisis* the conclusion that § 601 does not on its own terms reach disparate impact cases. However, the opinions adopting that conclusion did not engage in any independent analysis of the reach of § 601. Indeed, the only writing on this subject came from two of the five Members of the *Bakke* "majority," each of whom wrote separately to reject the remaining Justices' understanding of their opinions in *Bakke* and to insist that § 601 does in fact reach some instances of unintentional discrimination.[16] The Court's occasional rote invocation of this *Guardians* majority in later cases ought not obscure the fact that the question whether § 601 applies to disparate-impact claims has never been analyzed by this

---

[15] Of course, those five Justices divided over the application of the Equal Protection Clause—and by extension Title VI—to affirmative action cases. Therefore, it is somewhat strange to treat the opinions of those five Justices in *Bakke* as constituting a majority for any particular substantive interpretation of Title VI.

[16] The fact that Justices Marshall and White both felt that the opinion they coauthored in *Bakke* did not resolve the question whether Title VI on its face reaches disparate-impact claims belies the majority's assertion that *Bakke* "had drawn precisely that distinction," much less its implication that it would have been "absurd" to think otherwise.

Court on the merits.

In addition, these Title VI cases seemingly ignore the well-established principle of administrative law that is now most often described as the "*Chevron* doctrine." In most other contexts, when the agencies charged with administering a broadly-worded statute offer regulations interpreting that statute or giving concrete guidance as to its implementation, we treat their interpretation of the statute's breadth as controlling unless it presents an unreasonable construction of the statutory text. While there may be some dispute as to the boundaries of *Chevron* deference, it is paradigmatically appropriate when Congress has clearly delegated agencies the power to issue regulations with the force of law and established formal procedures for the promulgation of such regulations.

If we were writing on a blank slate, we might very well conclude that Chevron and similar cases decided both before and after Guardians provide the proper framework for understanding the structure of Title VI. Under such a reading there would be no incongruity between §§ 601 and 602. Instead, we would read § 602 as granting the federal agencies responsible for distributing federal funds the authority to issue regulations interpreting § 601 on the assumption that their construction will—if reasonable—be incorporated into our understanding of § 601's meaning.[19]

To resolve this case, however, it is unnecessary to answer the question whether our cases interpreting the reach of § 601 should be reinterpreted in light of *Chevron*. If one understands the relationship between §§ 601 and 602 through the prism of *either Chevron* or our prior Title VI cases, the question presented all but answers itself. If the regulations promulgated pursuant to § 602 are either an authoritative construction of § 601's meaning or prophylactic rules necessary to actualize the goals enunciated in § 601, then it makes no sense to differentiate between private actions to enforce § 601 and private actions to enforce § 602. There is but one private action to enforce Title VI, and we already know that such an action exists.[20]

---

[19] The legislative history strongly indicates that the Congress that adopted Title VI and the administration that proposed the statute intended that the agencies and departments would utilize the authority granted under § 602 to shape the substantive contours of § 601. For example, during the hearings that preceded the passage of the statute, Attorney General Kennedy agreed that the administrators of the various agencies would have the power to define "what constitutes discrimination" under Title VI and "what acts or omissions are to be forbidden." It was, in fact, concern for this broad delegation that inspired Congress to amend the pending bill to ensure that all regulations issued pursuant to Title VI would have to be approved by the President.

[20] The majority twice suggests that I "be[g] the question" whether a private right of action to enforce Title VI necessarily encompasses a right of action to enforce the regulations validly promulgated pursuant to the statute. As the above analysis demonstrates, I do no such thing. On the contrary, I demonstrate that the disparate-impact regulations promulgated pursuant to § 602 are—and have always been considered to be—an important part of an integrated remedial scheme intended to promote the statute's antidiscrimination goals. Given that fact, there is simply no logical or legal justification for differentiating between actions to enforce the regulations and actions to enforce the statutory text. Furthermore, as my integrated approach reflects the longstanding practice of this Court, it is the majority's largely unexplained assumption that a private right of action to enforce the disparate-impact regulations must be independently established that "begs the question."

III

The majority couples its flawed analysis of the structure of Title VI with an uncharitable understanding of the substance of the divide between those on this Court who are reluctant to interpret statutes to allow for private rights of action and those who are willing to do so if the claim of right survives a rigorous application of the criteria set forth in *Cort v. Ash*. As the majority narrates our implied right of action jurisprudence, the Court's shift to a more skeptical approach represents the rejection of a common-law judicial activism in favor of a principled recognition of the limited role of a contemporary "federal tribunal." According to its analysis, the recognition of an implied right of action when the text and structure of the statute do not absolutely compel such a conclusion is an act of judicial self-indulgence. As much as we would like to help those disadvantaged by discrimination, we must resist the temptation to pour ourselves "one last drink." To do otherwise would be to "ventur[e] beyond Congress's intent."

Overwrought imagery aside, it is the majority's approach that blinds itself to congressional intent. While it remains true that, if Congress intends a private right of action to support statutory rights, "the far better course is for it to specify as much when it creates those rights," its failure to do so does not absolve us of the responsibility to endeavor to discern its intent. In a series of cases since *Cort v. Ash*, we have laid out rules and developed strategies for this task.

The very existence of these rules and strategies assumes that we will sometimes find manifestations of an implicit intent to create such a right. * * *

Underlying today's opinion is the conviction that *Cannon* must be cabined because it exemplifies an "expansive rights-creating approach." But, as I have taken pains to explain, it was Congress, not the Court, that created the cause of action, and it was the Congress that later ratified the *Cannon* holding in 1986 and again in 1988.

In order to impose its own preferences as to the availability of judicial remedies, the Court today adopts a methodology that blinds itself to important evidence of congressional intent. It is one thing for the Court to ignore the import of our holding in Cannon, as the breadth of that precedent is a matter upon which reasonable jurists may differ. It is entirely another thing for the majority to ignore the reasoning of that opinion and the evidence contained therein, as those arguments and that evidence speak directly to the question at issue today. * * * *Cannon* carefully explained that both Title VI and Title IX were intended to benefit a particular class of individuals, that the purposes of the statutes would be furthered rather than frustrated by the implication of a private right of action, and that the legislative histories of the statutes support the conclusion that Congress intended such a right. Those conclusions and the evidence supporting them continue to have force today.

Similarly, if the majority is genuinely committed to deciphering congressional intent, its unwillingness to even consider evidence as to the context in which Congress legislated is perplexing. Congress does not legislate in a vacuum. As the respondent and the Government suggest, and as we have held several times, the objective manifestations of congressional intent to create a private right of action must be measured in light of the enacting Congress' expectations as to how the judiciary might evaluate the question.[23]

At the time Congress was considering Title VI, it was normal practice for the courts to infer that Congress intended a private right of action whenever it passed a statute designed to protect a particular class that did not contain enforcement mechanisms which would be thwarted by a private remedy. Indeed, the very year Congress adopted Title VI, this Court specifically stated that "it is the duty of the courts to be alert to provide such remedies as are necessary to make effective the congressional purpose." *J.I. Case Co. v. Borak* (1964). Assuming, as we must, that Congress was fully informed as to the state of the law, the contemporary context presents important evidence as to Congress' intent—evidence the majority declines to consider.

Ultimately, respect for Congress' prerogatives is measured in deeds, not words. Today, the Court coins a new rule, holding that a private cause of action to enforce a statute does not encompass a substantive regulation issued to effectuate that statute unless the regulation does nothing more than "authoritatively construe the statute itself." This rule might be proper if we were the kind of "common-law court" the majority decries, inventing private rights of action never intended by Congress. For if we are not construing a statute, we certainly may refuse to create a remedy for violations of federal regulations. But if we are faithful to the commitment to discerning congressional intent that all Members of this Court profess, the distinction is untenable. There is simply no reason to assume that Congress contemplated, desired, or adopted a distinction between regulations that merely parrot statutory text and broader regulations that are authorized by statutory text.

IV

Beyond its flawed structural analysis of Title VI and an evident antipathy toward implied rights of action, the majority offers little affirmative support for its conclusion that Congress did not intend to create a private remedy for violations of the Title VI regulations.[26] The Court offers essentially two reasons for its position. First, it attaches significance to the fact that the "rights-creating" language in § 601 that defines the classes protected by the statute is not repeated in

---

[23] Like any other type of evidence, contextual evidence may be trumped by other more persuasive evidence. Thus, the fact that, when evaluating older statutes, we have at times reached the conclusion that Congress did not imply a private right of action does not have the significance the majority suggests.

[26] The majority suggests that its failure to offer such support is irrelevant, because the burden is on the party seeking to establish the existence of an implied right of action. That response confuses apples and oranges. Undoubtedly, anyone seeking to bring a lawsuit has the burden of establishing that private individuals have the right to bring such a suit. However, once the courts have examined the statutory scheme under which the individual seeks to bring a suit and determined that a private right of action does exist, judges who seek to impose heretofore unrecognized limits on that right have a responsibility to offer reasoned arguments drawn from the text, structure, or history of that statute in order to justify such limitations. Moreover, in this case, the petitioners have marshaled substantial affirmative evidence that a private right of action exists to enforce Title VI and the regulations validly promulgated thereunder. It strikes me that it aids rather than hinders their case that this evidence is already summarized in an opinion of this Court.

§ 602. But, of course, there was no reason to put that language in § 602 because it is perfectly obvious that the regulations authorized by § 602 must be designed to protect precisely the same people protected by § 601. Moreover, it is self-evident that, linguistic niceties notwithstanding, any statutory provision whose stated purpose is to "effectuate" the eradication of racial and ethnic discrimination has as its "focus" those individuals who, absent such legislation, would be subject to discrimination.

Second, the Court repeats the argument advanced and rejected in *Cannon* that the express provision of a fund cut-off remedy "suggests that Congress intended to preclude others." In *Cannon*, we carefully explained why the presence of an explicit mechanism to achieve one of the statute's objectives (ensuring that federal funds are not used "to support discriminatory practices") does not preclude a conclusion that a private right of action was intended to achieve the statute's other principal objective ("to provide individual citizens effective protection against those practices"). In support of our analysis, we offered policy arguments, cited evidence from the legislative history, and noted the active support of the relevant agencies. In today's decision, the Court does not grapple with—indeed, barely acknowledges—our rejection of this argument in *Cannon*.

Like much else in its opinion, the present majority's unwillingness to explain its refusal to find the reasoning in *Cannon* persuasive suggests that today's decision is the unconscious product of the majority's profound distaste for implied causes of action rather than an attempt to discern the intent of the Congress that enacted Title VI of the Civil Rights Act of 1964. Its colorful disclaimer of any interest in "venturing beyond Congress's intent" has a hollow ring.

* * *

I respectfully dissent.

Notes and Questions

1. At the outset, note that the Court must deal with several distinct problems. First, it must consider the scope of the statutory protection under Title VI. All of the Justices, if for no other reason than *stare decisis*, take the position that the statute proscribes only intentional discrimination, not rules or practices that have a disparate impact. Second, the Court must ponder whether regulations that § 602 authorizes may legitimately address disparate impact. This question the majority explicitly declines to take up. Third, the Court must consider whether there is a private right of action to enforce the regulation upon which the plaintiff class relies.

a. With respect to the second question, in *Guardians* the Court took the position that it was permissible for agency regulations promulgated under the authority of § 602 to exceed the scope of protection offered by § 601. Here, Justice Scalia says the Court will not address the issue. Has the Court not implicitly addressed the issue when it moves to consideration of the third question? (Justice O'Connor, interestingly, concurred in the judgment in *Guardians* but argued that agency regulations could not legitimately exceed the scope of § 601.) For that matter, when the majority says on page 31 that there is no rights language in § 602, is that an explicit negative answer? If not, what is the meaning of that language? If so, should the Court never reach the third question because it is unnecessary to the decision?

b. In *City of Rome v. United States*, the Court decided that Congress could act against voting practices that have a discriminatory effect even though § 1 of the Fifteenth Amendment prohibits only intentional discrimination. Justice O'Connor agreed. Is her position in *Rome* inconsistent with her position in *Guardians*? How do you think she might distinguish the two cases to accommodate her two views, which are, after all, at least superficially incompatible?

2. How is it possible for the Court to view *Guardians* as reaffirming *Bakke*'s limited view of § 601 and yet that § 602 regulations may go further? Justice Scalia notes that five Justices took that position in *Guardians*, but goes on to argue that their statements are "in considerable tension" with the rule of *Bakke* and *Guardians*. Given that a majority of the Court took the position of which Justice Scalia clearly disapproves, should he really be making the point that *Guardians* is in considerable tension with itself?

3. Does the majority now say that henceforth there will be no implied rights of action in statutes for all purposes? Justice Scalia notes that "private rights of action must be created by Congress." Does this overrule *Cort v. Ash* and *Cannon v. University of Chicago*? Has Justice Scalia's position in *Thompson* (*see* pages 424-25 of the text) prevailed?

4. The majority also reiterates the point made in other cases (*e.g. Schweiker v. Chilicky*) that the fact that Congress has provided one remedy strongly suggests that Congress did not intend others to exist. This is, essentially, an application of the old maxim of statutory construction: *experssio unius, exclusio alterius*. Theoretically, that leaves open the possibility of an implied right of action if Congress has created no remedy at all. How often do you think Congress will create new rights without creating any sort of remedial device to enforce the intent of the statute?

5. Is the Court justified in viewing rights of action under the statute and under the regulations separately? Should the implication standards be the same, or should the Court be even more chary of implying private rights of action in regulations? Is it legitimate for an agency to create a private right of action, expressly or implicitly, in its regulations of Congress has not created one in the authorizing statute? If not, then should not that end the Court's consideration of this case? If so, does that shed light on the legitimacy of the Court's implying a private right of action in either the statute or the underlying regulations?

6. Justice Stevens argues that *Cannon* makes clear that the statute covers *all* prohibited discrimination. Does that beg the question?

7. Was *Cannon* a disparate-impact case? Reread note 2 in the Court's opinion, which is on page 406 of the text. If it was a disparate-impact case, does that weaken the majority's argument and strengthen Justice Stevens's?

Chapter 6

THE FEDERAL FORUM, THE FOURTEENTH AMENDMENT, AND THE CIVIL RIGHTS ACT OF 1871

B. THE FOURTEENTH AMENDMENT IN THE REMEDIAL SCHEME

3. OFFICIALS' IMMUNITIES

To be inserted on page 549 as new Note 9 a):

In *Saucier v. Katz*, ___ U.S. ___, 121 S.Ct. 2151, ___ L.Ed.2d ___ (2001), the Court took the opportunity to clarify the proper sequence of inquiry in a qualified immunity case and the purpose of having such immunity for officials. Saucier had arrested Katz when the latter protested at a speech being given by Vice President Gore at the Presidio Army Base in San Francisco. Katz filed a *Bivens* action against Saucier, a military police officer, alleging that Saucier used excessive force in effecting the arrest. The Ninth Circuit had set out a two-step inquiry: first, whether the right Katz asserted was clearly established, and second, whether the reasonable officer could have believed that his conduct was lawful. As Justice Kennedy, writing for the Court, characterized the second inquiry, "the reasonableness inquiry into excessive force meant that it [the court] need not consider aspects of qualified immunity, leaving the whole matter to the jury." The Supreme Court reversed. Justice Kennedy first reiterated that the *Harlow* qualified immunity is an immunity from suit, not simply an immunity from liability. It resembles the double jeopardy protection in that it is an entitlement not to face judicial proceedings at all. That, he said, is why the Court has emphasized the need to resolve qualified immunity questions at a threshold stage.

A court required to rule upon the qualified immunity issue must consider, then, this threshold question: Taken in the light most favorable to the party asserting the injury, do the facts alleged show the officer's conduct violated a constitutional right? This must be the initial inquiry. In the course of determining whether a constitutional right was violated on the premises alleged, a court might find it necessary to set forth principles which will become the basis for a holding that a right is clearly established. This is the process for the law's elaboration from case to case, and it is one reason for our insisting upon turning to the existence or nonexistence of a constitutional right as the first inquiry. The law might be deprived of this explanation were a court simply to skip ahead to the question whether the law clearly established that the officer's conduct was unlawful in the circumstances of the case.

If no constitutional right would have been violated were the allegations established, there is no necessity for further inquiries concerning qualified immunity. On the other hand, if a violation could be made out on a favorable view of the parties' submissions, the next, sequential step is to ask whether the right was clearly established. This inquiry, it is vital to note, must be undertaken in light of the specific context of the case, not as a broad general proposition, and it too serves to advance understanding of the law and to allow officers to avoid the burden of trial if qualified immunity is applicable.

In the course of the discussion, the Court reaffirmed *Anderson v. Creighton*'s point that an officer's use of force might be unreasonable for purposes of the Fourth Amendment but still within the scope of the *Harlow* qualified immunity. Rather than remanding to the lower courts for reconsideration based on the proper sequence of inquiry, the Court then proceeded, first to assume that the facts alleged made out a proper excessive force claim and second to examine the facts, declaring that there was no clearly established rule preventing Saucier from acting as he did and that a reasonable officer in his position might well have believed that the degree of force he employed was legitimate given the necessity of protecting the Vice President. Having determined that Saucier was entitled to qualified immunity, the Court remanded, presumably for the lower court to enter an order dismissing the case.

The Court essentially resolved the case on the papers originally filed with respect to Saucier's motion for summary judgment in the district court. A case like *Saucier* again raises the question of how much latitude a civil rights plaintiff should have to develop a factual record in an attempt to demonstrate that the official acted unreasonably. Does the Court's repeated emphasis on analysis with respect to the particular facts of the case suggest that plaintiffs should be entitled to engage in discovery prior to a defendant's motion for summary judgment? Do you think that is what the Court intends? If so, has the Court eroded much of the protection against the burdens of litigation that it meant in *Harlow* to establish? If not, is the Court's focus on the facts of the individual case slanted in favor of an official-defendant and the allegations that he is able to make supporting the summary judgment motion?

Chapter 7

THE ELEVENTH AMENDMENT

C. LESS THAN MEETS THE EYE

To be inserted on page 583 as new Note 5.1:

5.1. *Actions by States Against States*. The text of the Eleventh Amendment appears not to preclude suits for money damages in the federal courts by one state against another. Nonetheless, the example of *Hans v. Louisiana* and the cases that have followed it cautions one not to place too much faith in the words themselves. The Court recently clarified the effect of the Eleventh Amendment on state-*versus*-state actions. *Kansas v. Colorado*, ___ U.S. ___, 121 S.Ct. 2023, ___ L.Ed.2d ___ (2001), an original action in the Supreme Court arising out of a dispute under a bi-state water compact, rehearsed cases dating back to 1904 in which the Court had permitted damage actions between state plaintiffs and defendants. However, the Court pointed out that there is an even longer line of authority that prohibits a state from acting as a nominal plaintiff on behalf of individual claimants against another state. Thus, where bondholders assigned state-defaulted bonds to their home state but remained the beneficial owners of the bonds, the state action to recover the bond proceeds from the issuing state would not lie. Similarly, where individuals financed a state-*versus*-state action and the plaintiff state had agreed to divide the litigation proceeds proportionally among the individual who had suffered losses, the Court had refused to allow the action to proceed. *Kansas v. Colorado* might have appeared to be a middle case. A special master appointed by the Court took evidence and made recommendations to the Court, including one that suggested that the Court award Kansas money damages from Colorado for the latter's depletion of Arkansas River water available to Kansas. The master recommended that the Court calculate damages by Kansas's losses rather than by Colorado's gains from the unlawful depletion. The formula that he used included calculations based on losses by individual Kansas farmers. Colorado objected that this effectively converted the action into one by individuals against a state, with Kansas acting only as a litigation front for its citizens. A unanimous Court (on this point) disagreed. Noting that Kansas had financed and retained full control of the litigation, the Court distinguished the action from those where the state proceeded on behalf of individuals rather than in its own interest. Although Kansas's "right to control the disposition of any recovery of damages is entirely unencumbered," which might mean that Kansas would elect to distribute the damage award to injured individuals, the Court apparently regarded the lack of any formal, identifiable individual interest in or control of the litigation as dispositive. Query whether such a distinction will be effective or whether the Court has simply given potential plaintiff states an extended lesson in structuring litigation to avoid the Eleventh Amendment bar.

D. EXTENDING AND CABINING THE DOCTRINE: THE LIMITS OF LIMITS

To be inserted on page 626 immediately before Note 4:

The Court continues to exclude states from the realm of "persons" unless Congress makes it impossible for the Court to do so. In *Vermont Agency of Natural Resources v. United States ex rel. Stevens*, 529 U.S. 765, 120 S.Ct. 1858, 146 L.Ed.2d 836 (2000), a majority of the Court declined to construe "persons" in the False Claims Act as encompassing states. The majority relied upon the general presumption that sovereigns are unaffected by legislation, disagreeing with Justice Stevens's and Justice Souter's argument that the presumption applies only to legislative acts of the sovereign to be charged. The Court also declined to attribute meaning to "persons" based on the interaction of other sections of the False Claims Act.

By interpreting the False Claims Act as it did, the Court avoided a novel Eleventh Amendment issue. *Vermont Agency* was a *qui tam* action brought by Stevens, the relator. Vermont resisted the action on several grounds, one of them being that the Eleventh Amendment barred the action. That raised the question of whether the relator in some sense assumed the characteristics of the plaintiff United States for Eleventh Amendment purposes. The Eleventh Amendment, of course, has no effect on actions by the federal government against a state. Interestingly, in another section of the opinion, the Court held that the relator assumed the standing of the United States for injury-in-fact and redressability purposes, much as a subrogee has the standing of the subrogor.

Yet the Court's avoidance of the issue raises other questions. To the extent that the Amendment is jurisdictional, as the Court has often said, should the Court have considered an issue of statutory construction before deciding whether it had subject matter jurisdiction at all? The *Ashwander* admonition to avoid decision of constitutional questions whenever possible runs into the principle that a court must first decide its jurisdiction before proceeding to other issues in the case. On the other hand, if one can avoid jurisdictional issues as the Court appears to have done here, why did the Court decide the standing issue, also an Article III matter, before grappling with the statute?

To be inserted on page 630 immediately before College Savings Bank v. Florida Prepaid Postsecondary Education Expense Board:

Kimel v. Florida Board of Regents, 528 U.S. 62, 120 S.Ct. 631, 145 L.Ed.2d 522 (2000), confirmed that the Court will continue to take a critical look at legislation that Congress enacts pursuant to § 5 of the Fourteenth Amendment. The plaintiffs in these consolidated actions alleged that the states for which they worked had discriminated against them on the basis of age, in violation of the Age Discrimination in Employment Act. Although the Court had little difficulty concluding that Congress had been sufficiently explicit about abrogating the states' Eleventh Amendment immunity, it nonetheless upheld the states' Eleventh Amendment challenge to application of ADEA to them. Noting that age is not a suspect (or even quasi-suspect) classification, the Court went on to note that under the rational-basis test, the presence of a class-based rationale for the classification took the case outside of the Fourteenth Amendment. The majority took the position that it was permissible to use age as a "proxy" for other characteristics (competence, energy, productivity) in which the state had a legitimate interest, even if the classification was probably not correct in the majority of cases. This raises fascinating questions about how rational a measuring device is if it malfunctions more often than not, but those are questions for the Constitutional Law course.

To be inserted on page 631 immediately before Note 10:

Florida Prepaid appeared to leave the door open for Congress to legislate provided that it assembled a better legislative record to show that it was addressing a national problem. A five-to-four Court appeared substantially to close that door in *Board of Trustees of the University of Alabama v. Garrett*, 531 U.S. 356, 121 S.Ct. 955, 148 L.Ed.2d 866 (2001). In the Americans with Disabilities Act, Congress had permitted individual suits against states. Writing for the majority, Chief Justice Rehnquist noted that under the Fourteenth Amendment, Congress's § 5 enforcement power " 'includes the authority both to remedy and to deter violation of rights guaranteed thereunder by prohibiting a somewhat broader swath of conduct, including that which is not itself forbidden by the Amendment's text,' " citing and quoting *Kimel v. Florida Board of Regents*, 528 U.S. 62, 120 S.Ct. 631, 145 L.Ed.2d 522 (2000), and *City of Boerne v. Flores*, 521 U.S. 507, 117 S.Ct. 2157, 138 L.Ed.2d 624 (1997). However, the Court ruled, "§ 5 legislation reaching beyond the scope of § 1's actual guarantees must exhibit congruence and proportionality between the injury to be prevented or remedied and the means adopted to that end." (Internal quotation marks omitted.) Although Congress had heard testimony and assembled a lengthy record of many instances of state discrimination against people with disabilities, unlike in *Florida Prepaid* where the Court saw no extensive record, the majority found the record here insufficient nonetheless:

> Congress is the final authority as to desirable public policy, but in order to authorize private individuals to recover money damages against the States, there must be a pattern of discrimination by the States which violates the Fourteenth Amendment, and the remedy imposed by Congress must be congruent and proportional to the targeted violation.

Dissenting, Justices Breyer, Stevens, Souter and Ginsburg argued that the Court should afford Congress the same leeway when it legislates under § 5's "appropriate legislation" standard as the states receive under the rational-basis test for equal protection review, a lenient standard indeed. Further, the dissent argued that the Court had erred in disregarding extensive evidence of county and local governmental discrimination against disabled persons as a part of the record that Congress had assembled. The Court, said Justice Breyer, had created a new and particularly exacting method of evaluating congressional legislation. "In reviewing § 5 legislation, we have never required the sort of extensive investigation of each piece of evidence that the Court appears to contemplate. * * * Nor has the Court traditional required Congress to make findings as to state discrimination, or to break down the record evidence category by category." He assailed the majority on its new standard of review ("Rational-basis review—with its presumptions favoring constitutionality—is 'a paradigm of *judicial* restraint.' "), and accused it of abandoning the tradition of judicial deference to congressional legislation and retreating to a judicial approach reminiscent of the *Lochner* era. "The Court, through its evidentiary demands, its non-deferential review, and its failure to distinguish between judicial and legislative constitutional competencies, improperly invades a power that the Constitution assigns to Congress."

Irrespective of where one's sympathies lie in this debate, it is now clear that Congress must assemble a far more targeted and state-specific legislative record if it wishes to authorize federal suits against the states by individuals. Should the Court read the Eleventh Amendment to require Congress to go beyond the sort of record that ordinarily suffices to support legislation? Note, by the way, the metamorphosis in the Court's approach to such legislation. In the 1980s, in cases like *Atascadero State Hospital v. Scan-*

Ion, the Court's focus was on whether Congress was sufficiently specific that states were subject to suit. Congress learned that lesson, and the Court has now shifted from requiring that sort of specificity in an area of legislative competence to viewing such competence as subdivided for Eleventh Amendment purposes. There is no suggestion in the *Garrett* majority opinion that Congress overstepped itself in applying the Americans with Disabilities Act to county and local governmental units. The legislative record apparently satisfied the normal rational-basis review. With respect to the states, however, the Court appears to have shifted its analysis from whether Congress has competence based on the area being regulated to whether Congress has competence based on the parties to be regulated. Do you think those who wrote the Eleventh Amendment saw it as a limitation on the scope of congressional substantive legislation? In *Fitzpatrick v. Bitzer*, had Congress assembled the sort of legislative record that the modern Court demands?

[Handwritten note: KIMMELL & GARRETT — CAN C USE §5 OF 14TH 2 CREATE CAUSE OF ACTION AGAINST 11TH?]

Chapter 9

SUPREME COURT REVIEW OF STATE COURT DECISIONS

C. INSULATING STATE DECISIONS FROM SUPREME COURT REVIEW

1. WITH SUBSTANTIVE LAW

a. *Adequacy, Independence and Certainty*

To be inserted on page 876 as new Note 3.1:

3.1. The 2000 presidential election may have muddied the law a bit. In terms of its importance for federal courts doctrine, *Bush v. Palm Beach County Canvassing Board*, 531 U.S. 70, 121 S.Ct. 471, 148 L.Ed.2d 366 (2000), overshadows the more famous case, *Bush v. Gore*, 531 U.S. 98, 121 S.Ct. 525, 148 L.Ed.2d 388 (2000), which directly decided the election. In the earlier case, then-Governor George Bush sought review in the United States Supreme Court of an order of the Florida Supreme Court interpreting Florida election statutes to permit manual recounts of ballots and extending the time in which such recounts could occur beyond the time that the Florida Secretary of State had determined. Bush argued that the Florida decision ran afoul of two federal constitutional provisions. A *per curiam* Court noted the source of its power to review the Florida decision:

> As a general rule, this Court defers to a state court's interpretation of a state statute.[a] But in the case of a law enacted by a state legislature applicable not only to elections to state offices, but also to the selection of Presidential electors, the legislature is not acting solely under the authority given it by the people of the State, but by virtue of a direct grant of authority made under Art. II, § 1, cl. 2, of the United States Constitution.

Thus far, there are no surprises. The Court then discussed the opinion of the Florida Supreme Court, concluding that "After reviewing the opinion of the Florida Supreme Court, we find

> "that there is considerable uncertainty as to the precise grounds for the decision." *Minnesota v. National Tea Co.*, 309 U.S. 551, 555, 60 S.Ct. 676, 84 L.Ed. 920 (1940). This is sufficient reason for us to decline at this time to review the federal

---

[a] [EDITORS' NOTE] As an aside, is the Court entirely accurate in characterizing its normal approach as "deferring" to state courts? *Murdock v. Memphis* appears to stand for the proposition that on appeals from state courts, those courts speak with final authority on the *meaning* of state law, and the Supreme Court is without power to review such determinations except for constitutional infirmity. Is the Court suggesting that its deference is a matter of policy more than of jurisdiction?

50

questions asserted to be present. * * *

Specifically, we are unclear as to the extent to which the Florida Supreme Court saw the Florida Constitution as circumscribing the legislature's authority under Art. II, § 1, cl. 2. We are also unclear as to the consideration the Florida Supreme Court accorded to 3 U.S.C. § 5. The judgment of the Supreme Court of Florida is therefore vacated, and the case is remanded for further proceedings not inconsistent with this opinion.

Is the Court's reliance on *National Tea* and its remand for clarification of the precise grounds for the Florida Supreme Court's decision compatible with the position the Court took in *Michigan v. Long*? Recall that there, the majority (Justice O'Connor writing) ruled that if the grounds for a state supreme court's ruling were not clear, the Court would assume that the state court decided the way it did because of its perception that federal law compelled it to do so. On that assumption, the Supreme Court would hear the case on the merits, as it did in *Long*. Why does the Court not indulge the assumption in this case? Is *Bush v. Palm Beach County Canvassing Board* distinguishable in this respect from *Long*? To what extent does the third ground for remand that *National Tea* expressed still live?

Chapter 10

FEDERAL HABEAS CORPUS CHALLENGES TO STATE CUSTODY

E. RELITIGATING OLD CLAIMS

To be inserted on page 966 as Note 5:

5. The Supreme Court spoke on AEDPA's restrictions on evidentiary hearings in *Williams (Michael) v. Taylor*, 529 U.S. 420, 120 S.Ct. 1479, 146 L.Ed.2d 435 (2000), confirming *Cardwell v. Greene*'s view of the import of § 2254(e)(2)'s "failed to develop" language as denoting a fault-based consideration. The prisoner argued that the state had committed a *Brady* violation by failing to disclose the psychiatric report of the prisoner's co-defendant, who was the primary witness against him. He also argued that his trial was tainted by the presence of a juror who disclosed neither that she had been married to one of the prosecution's law enforcement witnesses for seventeen years nor that the prosecutor had represented her in the divorce proceeding. Finally, he argued that the prosecutor's failure to disclose those circumstances constituted prosecutorial misconduct.

The Fourth Circuit had ruled that the prisoner "failed to develop the factual basis" for his claims in the state proceedings, relying § 2254(e)(2). Although it rejected Virginia's no-fault interpretation of the statute, it ruled that the prisoner had not exercised due diligence with respect to the claims. A unanimous Supreme Court affirmed in part and reversed in part, reading the statute to codify the approach of *Keeney v. Tamayo-Reyes*, discussed at page 955 of the text, with the exception of eliminating *Keeney*'s "miscarriage of justice" exception to the established cause-and-prejudice standard. The Court upheld the Fourth Circuit's ruling with respect to the psychiatric report, on the ground that references to the report in the co-defendant's sentencing proceeding should have alerted Williams's counsel to the existence of the report as possible *Brady* material. Given that the state has an affirmative duty under *Brady* to turn over exculpatory material, and that the state's failure to do so is grounds for reversal on direct appeal, has Congress restricted the due process right that *Brady* represents in the context of habeas review? If so, does that raise any problems? If not, then is defendant's diligence relevant?

With respect to the second and third claims that Williams lodged, the Court ruled that Williams had met the burden of showing diligence. Williams relied on the juror's negative answers to two questions during *voir dire*. First, the court asked "Are any of you related to the following people who may be called as witnesses?" The court read the jurors a list of names, one of which was the juror's former husband of seventeen years with whom she had had four children. The juror did not respond. (In an affidavit submitted in conjunction with the federal habeas proceedings, the juror indicated that she did not consider herself any longer related to the witness; their marriage had ended fifteen years before the trial. The prosecutor also submitted an affidavit to the same effect.)

Second, the trial court asked, "Have you or any member of your immediate family ever been represented by any of the aforementioned attorneys?" The juror remained silent although the prosecutor had represented her in the divorce proceeding. The prosecutor also remained silent. The juror later explained that since the divorce was uncontested, she did not consider that the prosecutor was representing either her or her then-husband. The prosecutor stated that he no longer remembered the representation.

The Court refused to endorse either the conduct of the juror or the Fourth Circuit's application of the due-diligence standard that both courts read into the "failed to develop" language of § 2254(e)(2).

> Even if [the juror] had been correct in her technical or literal interpretation of the question relating to [the witness], her silence after the first question could suggest to the finder of fact an unwillingness to be forthcoming; this in turn could bear on the veracity of her explanation for not disclosing that [the prosecutor] had been her attorney. [The witness's] failure to divulge material information in response to the second question was misleading as a matter of fact because under any interpretation, [the prosecutor] had acted as counsel to her and [the witness] in their divorce. Coupled with [the prosecutor's] own reticence, these omissions as a whole disclose the need for an evidentiary hearing.

The Court disagreed with the Fourth Circuit that the trial record contained anything that should have put a reasonable defense attorney on notice that the juror's failure to respond to either of the two questions "was a deliberate omission of material information." In state habeas proceedings, Williams had attempted to investigate the circumstances surrounding empanelment of the jury, though the focus was on a different juror. However, Virginia opposed the effort and the Virginia Supreme Court cut it off, understandably in the eyes of the Supreme Court, given the vagueness of the prisoner's allegations. Federal habeas counsel only discovered the problem because two of the other jurors, while being interviewed by an investigator, happened to refer to the problem juror by her former, married name. The Virginia Supreme Court thought that, with due diligence, state habeas counsel could have discovered the same information. The Supreme Court disagreed: "Because of [the juror's] and [the prosecutor's] silence, there was no basis for an investigation into [the juror's] marriage history. Section 2254(e)(2) does not apply to petitioner's related claims of juror bias and prosecutorial misconduct."

F. RAISING NEW CLAIMS

2. NEW CLAIMS BASED ON NEW LAW

To be inserted on page 995 immediately before Note 4:

Edwards v. Carpenter, 529 U.S. 446, 120 S.Ct. 1587, 146 L.Ed.2d 518 (2000), caused (so to speak) the Court again to confront the relationship between ineffective-assistance claims and state procedural default. Perhaps not surprisingly, the Court held that ineffective assistance may satisfy the cause requirement for a procedurally defaulted claim, but the Court also added another layer to the analysis by holding that the prisoner may default the ineffective-assistance claim itself. In this event, the prisoner would have to seek state habeas relief based on the second default, showing cause and prejudice for defaulting the ineffective-assistance claim. If successful in that endeavor, the prisoner would still have the challenge of demonstrating cause and prejudice for the underlying constitutional claim. Thus, he would have to prove two levels of cause and prejudice. Justice Breyer and Stevens, although they concurred in the result, thought that the federal court should evaluate the defaulted ineffective-assistance claim in the first instance. The majority, on the other hand, viewed that possibility as an end run around *Murray v. Carrier*'s exhaustion requirement.

WILLIAMS (TERRY) v. TAYLOR
Supreme Court of the United States, 2000.
120 S.Ct. 1495, 146 L.Ed.2d 389.

JUSTICE STEVENS announced the judgment of the Court and delivered the opinion of the Court with respect to Parts, I, III, and IV, and an opinion with respect to Parts II and V.[*]

The questions presented are whether Terry Williams' constitutional right to the effective assistance of counsel as defined in *Strickland v. Washington*, was violated, and whether the judgment of the Virginia Supreme Court refusing to set aside his death sentence "was contrary to, or involved an unreasonable application of, clearly established Federal law, as determined by the Supreme Court of the United States," within the meaning of 28 U.S.C. § 2254(d)(1). We answer both questions affirmatively.

I

On November 3, 1985, Harris Stone was found dead in his residence on Henry Street in Danville, Virginia. Finding no indication of a struggle, local officials determined that the cause of death was blood alcohol poisoning, and the case was considered closed. Six months after Stone's death, Terry Williams, who was then incarcerated in the "I" unit of the city jail for an unrelated offense, wrote a letter to the police stating that he had killed " 'that man down on Henry Street' " and also stating that he " 'did it' " to that " 'lady down on West Green Street' " and was " 'very sorry.' " The letter was unsigned, but it closed with a reference to "I cell." The police readily identified Williams as its author, and, on April 25, 1986, they obtained several statements from him. In one Williams admitted that, after Stone refused to lend him " 'a couple of dollars,' " he had killed Stone with a mattock and took the money from his wallet. In September 1986, Williams was convicted of robbery and capital murder.

At Williams' sentencing hearing, the prosecution proved that Williams had been convicted of armed robbery in 1976 and burglary and grand larceny in 1982. The prosecution also introduced the written confessions that Williams had made in April. The prosecution described two auto thefts and two separate violent assaults on elderly victims perpetrated after the Stone murder. On December 4, 1985, Williams had started a fire outside one victim's residence before attacking and robbing him. On March 5, 1986, Williams had brutally assaulted an elderly woman on West Green Street—an incident he had mentioned in his letter to the police. That confession was particularly damaging because other evidence established that the woman was in a "vegetative state" and not expected to recover. Williams had also been convicted of arson for setting a fire in the jail while awaiting trial in this case. Two expert witnesses employed by the State testified that there was a "high probability" that Williams would pose a serious

---

[*] Justice Souter, Justice Ginsburg, and Justice Breyer join this opinion in its entirety. Justice O'Connor and Justice Kennedy join Parts I, III, and IV of this opinion.

continuing threat to society.

The evidence offered by Williams' trial counsel at the sentencing hearing consisted of the testimony of Williams' mother, two neighbors, and a taped excerpt from a statement by a psychiatrist. One of the neighbors had not been previously interviewed by defense counsel, but was noticed by counsel in the audience during the proceedings and asked to testify on the spot. The three witnesses briefly described Williams as a "nice boy" and not a violent person. The recorded psychiatrist's testimony did little more than relate Williams' statement during an examination that in the course of one of his earlier robberies, he had removed the bullets from a gun so as not to injure anyone.

In his cross-examination of the prosecution witnesses, Williams' counsel repeatedly emphasized the fact that Williams had initiated the contact with the police that enabled them to solve the murder and to identify him as the perpetrator of the recent assaults, as well as the car thefts. In closing argument, Williams' counsel characterized Williams' confessional statements as "dumb," but asked the jury to give weight to the fact that he had "turned himself in, not on one crime but on four * * * that the [police otherwise] would not have solved." The weight of defense counsel's closing, however, was devoted to explaining that it was difficult to find a reason why the jury should spare Williams' life.[2]

The jury found a probability of future dangerousness and unanimously fixed Williams' punishment at death. The trial judge concluded that such punishment was "proper" and "just" and imposed the death sentence. The Virginia Supreme Court affirmed the conviction and sentence. It rejected Williams' argument that when the trial judge imposed sentence, he failed to give mitigating weight to the fact that Williams had turned himself in.

State Habeas Corpus Proceedings

In 1988 Williams filed for state collateral relief in the Danville Circuit Court. The petition was subsequently amended, and the Circuit Court (the same judge who had presided over Williams' trial and sentencing) held an evidentiary hearing on Williams' claim that trial counsel had been ineffective.[3] Based on the evidence adduced after two days of hearings, Judge Ingram found that Williams' conviction was valid, but that his trial attorneys had been ineffective during sentencing. Among the evidence reviewed that had not been presented at trial were

---

[2] In defense counsel's words: "I will admit too that it is very difficult to ask you to show mercy to a man who maybe has not shown much mercy himself. I doubt very seriously that he thought much about mercy when he was in Mr. Stone's bedroom that night with him. I doubt very seriously that he had mercy very highly on his mind when he was walking along West Green and the incident with Alberta Stroud. I doubt very seriously that he had mercy on his mind when he took two cars that didn't belong to him. Admittedly it is very difficult to get us [*sic*, probably intending "up"] and ask that you give this man mercy when he has shown so little of it himself. But I would ask that you would."

[3] While Williams' petition was pending before the Circuit Court, Virginia amended its state habeas statute to vest in the State Supreme Court exclusive jurisdiction to award writs of habeas corpus in capital cases. Shortly after the Circuit Court held its evidentiary hearing, the Supreme Court assumed jurisdiction over Williams' petition and instructed the Circuit Court to issue findings of fact and legal recommendation[s] regarding Williams' ineffective-assistance claims.

documents prepared in connection with Williams' commitment when he was 11 years old that dramatically described mistreatment, abuse, and neglect during his early childhood, as well as testimony that he was "borderline mentally retarded," had suffered repeated head injuries, and might have mental impairments organic in origin. The habeas hearing also revealed that the same experts who had testified on the State's behalf at trial believed that Williams, if kept in a "structured environment," would not pose a future danger to society.

Counsel's failure to discover and present this and other significant mitigating evidence was "below the range expected of reasonable, professional competent assistance of counsel." Counsel's performance thus "did not measure up to the standard required under the holding of *Strickland*, and [if it had,] there is a reasonable probability that the result of the sentencing phase would have been different." Judge Ingram therefore recommended that Williams be granted a rehearing on the sentencing phase of his trial.

The Virginia Supreme Court did not accept that recommendation. Although it assumed, without deciding, that trial counsel had been ineffective, it disagreed with the trial judge's conclusion that Williams had suffered sufficient prejudice to warrant relief. Treating the prejudice inquiry as a mixed question of law and fact, the Virginia Supreme Court accepted the factual determination that available evidence in mitigation had not been presented at the trial, but held that the trial judge had misapplied the law in two respects. First, relying on our decision in *Lockhart v. Fretwell*, the court held that it was wrong for the trial judge to rely " 'on mere outcome determination' " when assessing prejudice. Second, it construed the trial judge's opinion as having "adopted a *per se* approach" that would establish prejudice whenever any mitigating evidence was omitted.

The court then reviewed the prosecution evidence supporting the "future dangerousness" aggravating circumstance, reciting Williams' criminal history, including the several most recent offenses to which he had confessed. In comparison, it found that the excluded mitigating evidence—which it characterized as merely indicating "that numerous people, mostly relatives, thought that defendant was nonviolent and could cope very well in a structured environment"— "barely would have altered the profile of this defendant that was presented to the jury." On this basis, the court concluded that there was no reasonable possibility that the omitted evidence would have affected the jury's sentencing recommendation, and that Williams had failed to demonstrate that his sentencing proceeding was fundamentally unfair.

Federal Habeas Corpus Proceedings

Having exhausted his state remedies, Williams sought a federal writ of habeas corpus. After reviewing the state habeas hearing transcript and the state courts' findings of fact and conclusions of law, the federal trial judge agreed with the Virginia trial judge: The death sentence was constitutionally infirm.

After noting that the Virginia Supreme Court had not addressed the question whether trial counsel's performance at the sentencing hearing fell below the range of competence demanded of lawyers in criminal cases, the judge began by addressing that issue in detail. He identified five categories of mitigating evidence that counsel had failed to introduce,[4] and he rejected the argument that counsel's failure to conduct an adequate investigation had been a strategic decision to rely almost entirely on the fact that Williams had voluntarily confessed.

According to Williams' trial counsel's testimony before the state habeas court, counsel did not fail to seek Williams' juvenile and social services records because he thought they would be counterproductive, but because counsel erroneously believed that " 'state law didn't permit it.' " Counsel also acknowledged in the course of the hearings that information about Williams' childhood would have been important in mitigation. And counsel's failure to contact a potentially persuasive character witness was likewise not a conscious strategic choice, but simply a failure to return that witness' phone call offering his service. Finally, even if counsel neglected to conduct such an investigation at the time as part of a tactical decision, the District Judge found, tactics as a matter of reasonable performance could not justify the omissions.

Turning to the prejudice issue, the judge determined that there was " 'a reasonable probability that, but for counsel's unprofessional errors, the result of the proceeding would have been different.' *Strickland*." He found that the Virginia Supreme Court had erroneously assumed that *Lockhart* had modified the *Strickland* standard for determining prejudice, and that it had made an important error of fact in discussing its finding of no prejudice.[5] Having introduced his analysis of Williams' claim with the standard of review applicable on habeas appeals provided by 28 U.S.C. § 2254(d), the judge concluded that those errors established that the Virginia Supreme Court's decision "was contrary to, or involved an unreasonable application of, clearly established Federal law" within the meaning of § 2254(d)(1).

The Federal Court of Appeals reversed. It construed § 2254(d)(1) as prohibiting the grant of habeas corpus relief unless the state court "decided the question by interpreting or applying the relevant precedent in a manner that reasonable jurists would all agree is unreasonable." Applying that standard, it could not

---

[4] (i) Counsel did not introduce evidence of the Petitioner's background * * *. (ii) Counsel did not introduce evidence that Petitioner was abused by his father. (iii) Counsel did not introduce testimony from correctional officers who were willing to testify that defendant would not pose a danger while incarcerated. Nor did counsel offer prison commendations awarded to Williams for his help in breaking up a prison drug ring and for returning a guard's wallet. (iv) Several character witnesses were not called to testify * * *. [T]he testimony of Elliott, a respected CPA in the community, could have been quite important to the jury * * *. (v) Finally, counsel did not introduce evidence that Petitioner was borderline mentally retarded, though he was found competent to stand trial.

[5] Specifically, the Virginia Supreme Court found no prejudice, reasoning: "The mitigation evidence that the prisoner says, in retrospect, his trial counsel should have discovered and offered barely would have altered the profile of this defendant that was presented to the jury. At most, this evidence would have shown that numerous people, mostly relatives, thought that defendant was nonviolent and could cope very well in a structured environment." The Virginia Supreme Court ignored or overlooked the evidence of Williams' difficult childhood and abuse and his limited mental capacity. It is also unreasonable to characterize the additional evidence as coming from "mostly relatives." As stated, Bruce Elliott, a respected professional in the community, and several correctional officers offered to testify on Williams behalf.

say that the Virginia Supreme Court's decision on the prejudice issue was an unreasonable application of the tests developed in either Strickland or Lockhart. It explained that the evidence that Williams presented a future danger to society was "simply overwhelming"; it endorsed the Virginia Supreme Court's interpretation of *Lockhart,* and it characterized the state court's understanding of the facts in this case as "reasonable."

We granted certiorari and now reverse.

II

In 1867, Congress enacted a statute providing that federal courts "shall have power to grant writs of habeas corpus in all cases where any person may be restrained of his or her liberty in violation of the constitution, or of any treaty or law of the United States * * * ." Over the years, the federal habeas corpus statute has been repeatedly amended, but the scope of that jurisdictional grant remains the same. It is, of course, well settled that the fact that constitutional error occurred in the proceedings that led to a state-court conviction may not alone be sufficient reason for concluding that a prisoner is entitled to the remedy of habeas. On the other hand, errors that undermine confidence in the fundamental fairness of the state adjudication certainly justify the issuance of the federal writ. The deprivation of the right to the effective assistance of counsel recognized in *Strickland* is such an error.

The warden here contends that federal habeas corpus relief is prohibited by the amendment to 28 U.S.C. § 2254, enacted as a part of the Antiterrorism and Effective Death Penalty Act of 1996 (AEDPA). The relevant portion of that amendment provides:

> (d) An application for a writ of habeas corpus on behalf of a person in custody pursuant to the judgment of a State court shall not be granted with respect to any claim that was adjudicated on the merits in State court proceedings unless the adjudication of the claim—

> (1) resulted in a decision that was contrary to, or involved an unreasonable application of, clearly established Federal law, as determined by the Supreme Court of the United States * * * .

In this case, the Court of Appeals applied the construction of the amendment that it had adopted in its earlier opinion in *Green v. French.* It read the amendment as prohibiting federal courts from issuing the writ unless:

> (a) the state court decision is in "square conflict" with Supreme Court precedent that is controlling as to law and fact or (b) if no such controlling decision exists, the state court's resolution of a question of pure law rests upon an objectively unreasonable derivation of legal principles from the relevant [S]upreme [C]ourt precedents, or if its decision rests upon an objectively unreasonable application of established principles to new facts.

Accordingly, it held that a federal court may issue habeas relief only if "the state courts have decided the question by interpreting or applying the relevant precedent in a manner that reasonable jurists would all agree is unreasonable."

We are convinced that that interpretation of the amendment is incorrect. It would impose a test for determining when a legal rule is clearly established that simply cannot be squared with the real practice of decisional law.[9] It would apply a standard for determining the "reasonableness" of state-court decisions that is not contained in the statute itself, and that Congress surely did not intend. And it would wrongly require the federal courts, including this Court, to defer to state judges' interpretations of federal law.

As the Fourth Circuit would have it, a state-court judgment is "unreasonable" in the face of federal law only if all reasonable jurists would agree that the state court was unreasonable. Thus, in this case, for example, even if the Virginia Supreme Court misread our opinion in Lockhart, we could not grant relief unless we believed that none of the judges who agreed with the state court's interpretation of that case was a "reasonable jurist." But the statute says nothing about "reasonable judges," presumably because all, or virtually all, such judges occasionally commit error; they make decisions that in retrospect may be characterized as "unreasonable." Indeed, it is most unlikely that Congress would deliberately impose such a requirement of unanimity on federal judges. As Congress is acutely aware, reasonable lawyers and lawgivers regularly disagree with one another. Congress surely did not intend that the views of one such judge who might think that relief is not warranted in a particular case should always have greater weight than the contrary, considered judgment of several other reasonable judges.

The inquiry mandated by the amendment relates to the way in which a federal habeas court exercises its duty to decide constitutional questions; the amendment does not alter the underlying grant of jurisdiction in § 2254(a).[10] When federal judges exercise their federal-question jurisdiction under the "judicial Power" of Article III of the Constitution, it is "emphatically the province and duty" of those judges to "say what the law is." At the core of this power is the federal courts' independent responsibility— independent from its coequal

---

[9] Although we explain our understanding of "clearly established law," we note that the Fourth Circuit's construction of the amendment's inquiry in this respect is especially problematic. It separates cases into those for which a "controlling decision" exists and those for which no such decision exists. The former category includes very few cases, since a rule is "controlling" only if it matches the case before the court both "as to law and fact," and most cases are factually distinguishable in some respect. A literal application of the Fourth Circuit test would yield a particularly perverse outcome in cases involving the *Strickland* rule for establishing ineffective assistance of counsel, since that case, which established the "controlling" rule of law on the issue, contained facts insufficient to show ineffectiveness.

[10] Indeed, Congress roundly rejected an amendment to the bill eventually adopted that directly invoked the text of the jurisdictional grant, 28 U.S.C. § 2254(a) (providing that the federal courts "shall entertain an application for a writ of habeas corpus" (emphasis added)). The amendment read: "Notwithstanding any other provision of law, an application for a writ of habeas corpus in behalf of a person in custody pursuant to a judgment or order of a State court shall not be entertained by a court of the United States unless the remedies in the courts of the State are inadequate or ineffective to test the legality of the person's detention." ([A]mendment of Sen. Kyl) (emphasis added). In speaking against the Kyl amendment, Senator Specter (a key proponent of the eventual habeas reform) explained that when "dealing with the question of jurisdiction of the Federal courts to entertain questions on Federal issues, on constitutional issues, I believe it is necessary that the Federal courts retain that jurisdiction as a constitutional matter."

branches in the Federal Government, and independent from the separate authority of the several States—to interpret federal law. A construction of AEDPA that would require the federal courts to cede this authority to the courts of the States would be inconsistent with the practice that federal judges have traditionally followed in discharging their duties under Article III of the Constitution. If Congress had intended to require such an important change in the exercise of our jurisdiction, we believe it would have spoken with much greater clarity than is found in the text of AEDPA.

This basic premise informs our interpretation of both parts of § 2254(d)(1): first, the requirement that the determinations of state courts be tested only against "clearly established Federal law, as determined by the Supreme Court of the United States," and second, the prohibition on the issuance of the writ unless the state court's decision is "contrary to, or involved an unreasonable application of," that clearly established law. We address each part in turn.

The "clearly established law" requirement

In *Teague v. Lane*, we held that the petitioner was not entitled to federal habeas relief because he was relying on a rule of federal law that had not been announced until after his state conviction became final. The antiretroactivity rule recognized in Teague, which prohibits reliance on "new rules," is the functional equivalent of a statutory provision commanding exclusive reliance on "clearly established law." Because there is no reason to believe that Congress intended to require federal courts to ask both whether a rule sought on habeas is "new" under Teague—which remains the law—and also whether it is "clearly established" under AEDPA, it seems safe to assume that Congress had congruent concepts in mind. It is perfectly clear that AEDPA codifies Teague to the extent that Teague requires federal habeas courts to deny relief that is contingent upon a rule of law not clearly established at the time the state conviction became final.[12]

Teague's core principles are therefore relevant to our construction of this requirement. Justice Harlan recognized the "inevitable difficulties" that come with "attempting 'to determine whether a particular decision has really announced a "new" rule at all or whether it has simply applied a well-established

---

[12] We are not persuaded by the argument that because Congress used the words "clearly established law" and not "new rule," it meant in this section to codify an aspect of the doctrine of executive qualified immunity rather than *Teague*'s antiretroactivity bar. The warden refers us specifically to § 2244(b)(2)(A) and 28 U.S.C. § 2254(e)(2), in which the statute does in so many words employ the "new rule" language familiar to *Teague* and its progeny. Congress thus knew precisely the words to use if it had wished to codify *Teague per se*. That it did not use those words in § 2254(d) is evidence, the argument goes, that it had something else in mind entirely in amending that section. We think, quite the contrary, that the verbatim adoption of the *Teague* language in these other sections bolsters our impression that Congress had *Teague*—and not any unrelated area of our jurisprudence—specifically in mind in amending the habeas statute. These provisions, seen together, make it impossible to conclude that Congress was not fully aware of, and interested in codifying into law, that aspect of this Court's habeas doctrine. We will not assume that in a single subsection of an amendment entirely devoted to the law of habeas corpus, Congress made the anomalous choice of reaching into the doctrinally distinct law of qualified immunity, for a single phrase that just so happens to be the conceptual twin of a dominant principle in habeas law of which Congress was fully aware.

constitutional principle to govern a case which is closely analogous to those which have been previously considered in the prior case law.'" But *Teague* established some guidance for making this determination, explaining that a federal habeas court operates within the bounds of comity and finality if it applies a rule "dictated by precedent existing at the time the defendant's conviction became final." ([E]mphasis deleted). A rule that "breaks new ground or imposes a new obligation on the States or the Federal Government," falls outside this universe of federal law.

To this, AEDPA has added, immediately following the "clearly established law" requirement, a clause limiting the area of relevant law to that "determined by the Supreme Court of the United States." If this Court has not broken sufficient legal ground to establish an asked-for constitutional principle, the lower federal courts cannot themselves establish such a principle with clarity sufficient to satisfy the AEDPA bar. In this respect, we agree with the Seventh Circuit that this clause "extends the principle of *Teague* by limiting the source of doctrine on which a federal court may rely in addressing the application for a writ."

* * *

A rule that fails to satisfy the foregoing criteria is barred by *Teague* from application on collateral review, and, similarly, is not available as a basis for relief in a habeas case to which AEDPA applies.

In the context of this case, we also note that, as our precedent interpreting *Teague* has demonstrated, rules of law may be sufficiently clear for habeas purposes even when they are expressed in terms of a generalized standard rather than as a bright-line rule. As Justice Kennedy has explained:

> If the rule in question is one which of necessity requires a case-by-case examination of the evidence, then we can tolerate a number of specific applications without saying that those applications themselves create a new rule * * *. Where the beginning point is a rule of this general application, a rule designed for the specific purpose of evaluating a myriad of factual contexts, it will be the infrequent case that yields a result so novel that it forges a new rule, one not dictated by precedent.

Moreover, the determination whether or not a rule is clearly established at the time a state court renders its final judgment of conviction is a question as to which the "federal courts must make an independent evaluation."

It has been urged, in contrast, that we should read *Teague* and its progeny to encompass a broader principle of deference requiring federal courts to "validat[e] 'reasonable, good-faith interpretations' of the law" by state courts. The position has been bolstered with references to our statements elucidating the "new rule" inquiry as one turning on whether "reasonable jurists" would agree the rule was not clearly established. This presumption of deference was in essence the position taken by three Members of this Court in *Wright* (opinion of Thomas, J.) ("[A] federal habeas court must defer to the state court's decision rejecting the claim unless that decision is patently unreasonable.").

Teague, however, does not extend this far. The often repeated language that *Teague* endorses "reasonable, good-faith interpretations" by state courts is an explanation of policy, not a statement of law. The *Teague* cases reflect this Court's view that habeas corpus is not to be used as a second criminal trial, and federal courts are not to run roughshod over the considered findings and judgments of the state courts that conducted the original trial and heard the initial appeals. On the contrary, we have long insisted that federal habeas courts attend closely to those considered decisions, and give them full effect when their findings and judgments are consistent with federal law. But as Justice O'Connor explained in *Wright*:

> [T]he duty of the federal court in evaluating whether a rule is "new" is not the same as deference; * * * *Teague* does not direct federal courts to spend less time or effort scrutinizing the existing federal law, on the ground that they can assume the state courts interpreted it properly.

> [T]he maxim that federal courts should "give great weight to the considered conclusions of a coequal state judiciary" * * * does not mean that we have held in the past that federal courts must presume the correctness of a state court's legal conclusions on habeas, or that a state court's incorrect legal determination has ever been allowed to stand because it was reasonable. We have always held that federal courts, even on habeas, have an independent obligation to say what the law is.

We are convinced that in the phrase, "clearly established law," Congress did not intend to modify that independent obligation.

The "contrary to, or an unreasonable application of," requirement

The message that Congress intended to convey by using the phrases, "contrary to" and "unreasonable application of" is not entirely clear. The prevailing view in the Circuits is that the former phrase requires *de novo* review of "pure" questions of law and the latter requires some sort of "reasonability" review of so-called mixed questions of law and fact.

We are not persuaded that the phrases define two mutually exclusive categories of questions. Most constitutional questions that arise in habeas corpus proceedings—and therefore most "decisions" to be made—require the federal judge to apply a rule of law to a set of facts, some of which may be disputed and some undisputed. For example, an erroneous conclusion that particular circumstances established the voluntariness of a confession, or that there exists a conflict of interest when one attorney represents multiple defendants, may well be described either as "contrary to" or as an "unreasonable application of" the governing rule of law. In constitutional adjudication, as in the common law, rules of law often develop incrementally as earlier decisions are applied to new factual situations. But rules that depend upon such elaboration are hardly less lawlike than those that establish a bright-line test.

Indeed, our pre-AEDPA efforts to distinguish questions of fact, questions of law, and "mixed questions," and to create an appropriate standard of habeas review for each, generated some not insubstantial differences of opinion as to which issues of law fell into which category of question, and as to which standard of review applied to each. We thus think the Fourth Circuit was correct when it attributed the lack of clarity in the statute, in part, to the overlapping meanings of the phrases "contrary to" and "unreasonable application of."

The statutory text likewise does not obviously prescribe a specific, recognizable standard of review for dealing with either phrase. Significantly, it does not use any term, such as "de novo" or "plain error," that would easily identify a familiar standard of review. Rather, the text is fairly read simply as a command that a federal court not issue the habeas writ unless the state court was wrong as a matter of law or unreasonable in its application of law in a given case. The suggestion that a wrong state-court "decision"—a legal judgment rendered "after consideration of *facts, and* * * * *law*," BLACK'S LAW DICTIONARY 407 (6th ed.1990) (emphasis added)—may no longer be redressed through habeas (because it is unreachable under the "unreasonable application" phrase) is based on a mistaken insistence that the § 2254(d)(1) phrases have not only independent, but mutually exclusive, meanings. Whether or not a federal court can issue the writ "under [the] 'unreasonable application' clause," the statute is clear that habeas may issue under § 2254(d)(1) if a state court "decision" is "contrary to * * * clearly established Federal law." We thus anticipate that there will be a variety of cases, like this one, in which both phrases may be implicated.

Even though we cannot conclude that the phrases establish "a body of rigid rules," they do express a "mood" that the federal judiciary must respect. In this respect, it seems clear that Congress intended federal judges to attend with the utmost care to state-court decisions, including all of the reasons supporting their decisions, before concluding that those proceedings were infected by constitutional error sufficiently serious to warrant the issuance of the writ. Likewise, the statute in a separate provision provides for the habeas remedy when a state-court decision "was based on an unreasonable determination of the facts *in light of the evidence presented in the State court proceeding*." ([E]mphasis added). While this provision is not before us in this case, it provides relevant context for our interpretation of § 2254(d)(1); in this respect, it bolsters our conviction that federal habeas courts must make as the starting point of their analysis the state courts' determinations of fact, including that aspect of a "mixed question" that rests on a finding of fact. AEDPA plainly sought to ensure a level of "deference to the determinations of state courts," provided those determinations did not conflict with federal law or apply federal law in an unreasonable way. Congress wished to curb delays, to prevent "retrials" on federal habeas, and to give effect to state convictions to the extent possible under law. When federal courts are able to fulfill these goals within the bounds of the law, AEDPA instructs them to do so.

On the other hand, it is significant that the word "deference" does not appear in the text of the statute itself. Neither the legislative history, nor the statutory text, suggests any difference in the so-called "deference" depending on which of the two phrases is implicated.[13] Whatever "deference" Congress had in

---

[13] As Judge Easterbrook has noted, the statute surely does not require the kind of "deference" appropriate in other contexts: "It does not tell us to 'defer' to state decisions, as if the Constitution means one thing in Wisconsin and another in Indiana. Nor does it tell us to treat state

mind with respect to both phrases, it surely is not a requirement that federal courts actually defer to a state-court application of the federal law that is, in the independent judgment of the federal court, in error. As Judge Easterbrook noted with respect to the phrase "contrary to": "Section 2254(d) requires us to give state courts' opinions a respectful reading, and to listen carefully to their conclusions, but when the state court addresses a legal question, it is the law 'as determined by the Supreme Court of the United States' that prevails."[14]

Our disagreement with Justice O'Connor about the precise meaning of the phrase "contrary to," and the word "unreasonable," is, of course, important, but should affect only a narrow category of cases. The simplest and first definition of "contrary to" as a phrase is "in conflict with." In this sense, we think the phrase surely capacious enough to include a finding that the state-court "decision" is simply "erroneous" or wrong. (We hasten to add that even "diametrically different" from, or "opposite" to, an established federal law would seem to include "decisions" that are wrong in light of that law.) And there is nothing in the phrase "contrary to"—as Justice O'Connor appears to agree—that implies anything less than independent review by the federal courts. Moreover, state-court decisions that do not "conflict" with federal law will rarely be "unreasonable" under either her reading of the statute or ours. We all agree that

---

courts the way we treat federal administrative agencies. Deference * * * depends on delegation. Congress did not delegate interpretive or executive power to the state courts. They exercise powers under their domestic law, constrained by the Constitution of the United States. 'Deference' to the jurisdictions bound by those constraints is not sensible."

[14] The Court advances three reasons for adopting its alternative construction of the phrase "unreasonable application of." First, the use of the word "unreasonable" in the statute suggests that Congress was directly influenced by the "patently unreasonable" standard advocated by Justice Thomas in his opinion in *Wright v. West*; second, the legislative history supports this view; and third, Congress must have intended to change the law more substantially than our reading 28 U.S.C. § 2254(d)(1) permits.

None of these reasons is persuasive. First, even though, as the Court recognizes, the term "unreasonable" is "difficult to define," neither the statute itself nor the Court's explanation of it, suggests that AEDPA's "unreasonable application of" has the same meaning as Justice Thomas' " 'patently unreasonable' " standard mentioned in his dictum in *Wright*. To the extent the "broader debate" in *Wright* touched upon the Court's novel distinction today between what is "wrong" and what is "unreasonable," it was in the context of a discussion not about the *standard of review* habeas courts should use for law-application questions, but about whether a rule is "new" or "old" such that *Teague*'s retroactivity rule would bar habeas relief; Justice Thomas contended that *Teague* barred habeas "whenever the state courts have interpreted old precedents *reasonably*, not [as Justice O'Connor suggested] only when they have done so 'properly.' " *Teague*, of course, as Justice O'Connor correctly pointed out, "did not establish a standard of review at all"; rather than instructing a court how to review a claim, it simply asks, in absolute terms, *whether* a rule was clear at the time of a state-court decision. We thus do not think *Wright* "confirms" anything about the meaning of § 2254(d)(1), which is, as our division reflects, anything but "clear."

As for the other bases for Justice O'Connor's view, the only two specific citations to the legislative history upon which she relies do no more than beg the question. One merely quotes the language of the statute without elaboration, and the other goes to slightly greater length in stating that state-court judgments must be upheld unless "unreasonable." Neither sheds any light on what the content of the hypothetical category of "decisions" that are wrong but nevertheless not "unreasonable." Finally, while we certainly agree with the Court that AEDPA wrought substantial changes in habeas law, there is an obvious fallacy in the assumption that because the statute changed pre-existing law in some respects, it must have rendered this specific change here.

state-court judgments must be upheld unless, after the closest examination of the state-court judgment, a federal court is firmly convinced that a federal constitutional right has been violated. Our difference is as to the cases in which, at first-blush, a state-court judgment seems entirely reasonable, but thorough analysis by a federal court produces a firm conviction that that judgment is infected by constitutional error. In our view, such an erroneous judgment is "unreasonable" within the meaning of the act even though that conclusion was not immediately apparent.

In sum, the statute directs federal courts to attend to every state-court judgment with utmost care, but it does not require them to defer to the opinion of every reasonable state-court judge on * * * federal law. If, after carefully weighing all the reasons for accepting a state court's judgment, a federal court is convinced that a prisoner's custody—or, as in this case, his sentence of death—violates the Constitution, that independent judgment should prevail. Otherwise the federal "law as determined by the Supreme Court of the United States" might be applied by the federal courts one way in Virginia and another way in California. In light of the well-recognized interest in ensuring that federal courts interpret federal law in a uniform way,[15] we are convinced that Congress did not intend the statute to produce such a result.

III

In this case, Williams contends that he was denied his constitutionally guaranteed right to the effective assistance of counsel when his trial lawyers failed to investigate and to present substantial mitigating evidence to the sentencing jury. The threshold question under AEDPA is whether Williams seeks to apply a rule of law that was clearly established at the time his state-court conviction became final. That question is easily answered because the merits of his claim are squarely governed by our holding in *Strickland*.

We explained in *Strickland* that a violation of the right on which Williams relies has two components:

> First, the defendant must show that counsel's performance was deficient. This requires showing that counsel made errors so serious that counsel was not functioning as the "counsel" guaranteed the defendant by the Sixth Amendment. Second, the defendant must show that the deficient performance prejudiced the defense. This requires showing that counsel's errors were so serious as to deprive the defendant of a fair trial, a trial whose result is reliable.

To establish ineffectiveness, a "defendant must show that counsel's representation fell below an objective standard of reasonableness." To establish

---

[15] Indeed, a contrary rule would be in substantial tension with the interest in uniformity served by Congress' modification in AEDPA of our previous Teague jurisprudence—now the law on habeas review must be "clearly established" by this Court alone. See supra, at 1506. It would thus seem somewhat perverse to ascribe to Congress the entirely inconsistent policy of perpetuating disparate readings of our decisions under the guise of deference to anything within a conceivable spectrum of reasonableness.

prejudice he "must show that there is a reasonable probability that, but for counsel's unprofessional errors, the result of the proceeding would have been different. A reasonable probability is a probability sufficient to undermine confidence in the outcome."

It is past question that the rule set forth in *Strickland* qualifies as "clearly established Federal law, as determined by the Supreme Court of the United States." That the *Strickland* test "of necessity requires a case-by-case examination of the evidence," obviates neither the clarity of the rule nor the extent to which the rule must be seen as "established" by this Court. This Court's precedent "dictated" that the Virginia Supreme Court apply the *Strickland* test at the time that court entertained Williams' ineffective-assistance claim. And it can hardly be said that recognizing the right to effective counsel "breaks new ground or imposes a new obligation on the States." Williams is therefore entitled to relief if the Virginia Supreme Court's decision rejecting his ineffective-assistance claim was either "contrary to, or involved an unreasonable application of," that established law. It was both.

IV

The Virginia Supreme Court erred in holding that our decision in *Lockhart v. Fretwell* modified or in some way supplanted the rule set down in *Strickland*. It is true that while the *Strickland* test provides sufficient guidance for resolving virtually all ineffective-assistance-of-counsel claims, there are situations in which the overriding focus on fundamental fairness may affect the analysis. Thus, on the one hand, as *Strickland* itself explained, there are a few situations in which prejudice may be presumed. And, on the other hand, there are also situations in which it would be unjust to characterize the likelihood of a different outcome as legitimate "prejudice." Even if a defendant's false testimony might have persuaded the jury to acquit him, it is not fundamentally unfair to conclude that he was not prejudiced by counsel's interference with his intended perjury.

Similarly, in *Lockhart*, we concluded that, given the overriding interest in fundamental fairness, the likelihood of a different outcome attributable to an incorrect interpretation of the law should be regarded as a potential "windfall" to the defendant rather than the legitimate "prejudice" contemplated by our opinion in *Strickland*. The death sentence that Arkansas had imposed on Bobby Ray Fretwell was based on an aggravating circumstance (murder committed for pecuniary gain) that duplicated an element of the underlying felony (murder in the course of a robbery). Shortly before the trial, the United States Court of Appeals for the Eighth Circuit had held that such "double counting" was impermissible, but Fretwell's lawyer (presumably because he was unaware of the * * * decision) failed to object to the use of the pecuniary gain aggravator. Before Fretwell's claim for federal habeas corpus relief reached this Court, the case was overruled. Accordingly, even though the Arkansas trial judge probably would have sustained a timely objection to the double counting, it had become clear that the State had a right to rely on the disputed aggravating circumstance. Because the ineffectiveness of Fretwell's counsel had not deprived him of any substantive or procedural right to which the law entitled him, we held that his claim did not satisfy the "prejudice" component of the Strickland test.

Cases such as *Nix v. Whiteside* and *Lockhart v. Fretwell* do not justify a departure from a straightforward application of *Strickland* when the ineffectiveness of counsel does deprive the defendant of a substantive or procedural right to which the law entitles him.[18] In the instant case, it is undisputed that Williams had a right—indeed, a constitutionally protected right—to provide the jury with the mitigating evidence that his trial counsel either failed to discover or failed to offer.

Nevertheless, the Virginia Supreme Court read our decision in *Lockhart* to require a separate inquiry into fundamental fairness even when Williams is able to show that his lawyer was ineffective and that his ineffectiveness probably affected the outcome of the proceeding. It wrote:

> The prisoner argues there "is a 'reasonable probability' that at least one juror would have been moved to spare Petitioner's life had he heard" the mitigation evidence developed at the habeas hearing that was not presented at the trial. Summarizing, he contends there "is a 'reasonable probability' that had at least one juror heard any of this evidence—let alone all of this evidence—the outcome of this case would have been different."
>
> We reject these contentions. The prisoner's discussion flies in the face of the Supreme Court's admonition in *Lockhart* that "an analysis focusing solely on mere outcome determination, without attention to whether the result of the proceeding was fundamentally unfair or unreliable, is defective."

Unlike the Virginia Supreme Court, the state trial judge omitted any reference to *Lockhart* and simply relied on our opinion in *Strickland* as stating the correct standard for judging ineffective-assistance claims. With respect to the prejudice component, he wrote:

> Even if a Petitioner shows that counsel's performance was deficient, however, he must also show prejudice. Petitioner must show "that there is a reasonable probability that but for counsel's unprofessional errors, the result * * * would have been different." "A reasonable probability is a probability sufficient to undermine confidence in the outcome." Indeed, it is insufficient to show only that the errors had some conceivable effect on the outcome of the proceeding, because virtually every act or omission of counsel would meet that test. The petitioner bears the "highly demanding" and "heavy burden" in establishing actual prejudice.

The trial judge analyzed the ineffective-assistance claim under the correct standard; the Virginia Supreme Court did not.

---

[18] In her concurring opinion in *Lockhart*, Justice O'Connor stressed this precise point.

I write separately only to point out that today's decision will, in the vast majority of cases, have no effect on the prejudice inquiry under *Strickland*. The determinative question—whether there is "a reasonable probability that, but for counsel's unprofessional errors, the result of the proceeding would have been different,"—remains unchanged. This case, however, concerns the unusual circumstance where the defendant attempts to demonstrate prejudice based on considerations that, as a matter of law, ought not inform the inquiry.

We are likewise persuaded that the Virginia trial judge correctly applied both components of that standard to Williams' ineffectiveness claim. Although he concluded that counsel competently handled the guilt phase of the trial, he found that their representation during the sentencing phase fell short of professional standards—a judgment barely disputed by the State in its brief to this Court. The record establishes that counsel did not begin to prepare for that phase of the proceeding until a week before the trial. They failed to conduct an investigation that would have uncovered extensive records graphically describing Williams' nightmarish childhood, not because of any strategic calculation but because they incorrectly thought that state law barred access to such records. Had they done so, the jury would have learned that Williams' parents had been imprisoned for the criminal neglect of Williams and his siblings, that Williams had been severely and repeatedly beaten by his father, that he had been committed to the custody of the social services bureau for two years during his parents' incarceration (including one stint in an abusive foster home), and then, after his parents were released from prison, had been returned to his parents' custody.

Counsel failed to introduce available evidence that Williams was "borderline mentally retarded" and did not advance beyond sixth grade in school. They failed to seek prison records recording Williams' commendations for helping to crack a prison drug ring and for returning a guard's missing wallet, or the testimony of prison officials who described Williams as among the inmates "least likely to act in a violent, dangerous or provocative way." Counsel failed even to return the phone call of a certified public accountant who had offered to testify that he had visited Williams frequently when Williams was incarcerated as part of a prison ministry program, that Williams "seemed to thrive in a more regimented and structured environment," and that Williams was proud of the carpentry degree he earned while in prison.

Of course, not all of the additional evidence was favorable to Williams. The juvenile records revealed that he had been thrice committed to the juvenile system—for aiding and abetting larceny when he was 11 years old, for pulling a false fire alarm when he was 12, and for breaking and entering when he was 15. But as the Federal District Court correctly observed, the failure to introduce the comparatively voluminous amount of evidence that did speak in Williams' favor was not justified by a tactical decision to focus on Williams' voluntary confession. Whether or not those omissions were sufficiently prejudicial to have affected the outcome of sentencing, they clearly demonstrate that trial counsel did not fulfill their obligation to conduct a thorough investigation of the defendant's background.

We are also persuaded, unlike the Virginia Supreme Court, that counsel's unprofessional service prejudiced Williams within the meaning of Strickland. After hearing the additional evidence developed in the postconviction proceedings, the very judge who presided at Williams' trial and who once determined that the death penalty was "just" and "appropriate," concluded that there existed "a reasonable probability that the result of the sentencing phase would have been different" if the jury had heard that evidence. We do not agree with the Virginia Supreme Court that Judge Ingram's conclusion should be discounted because he apparently adopted "a *per se* approach to the prejudice element" that placed undue "emphasis on mere outcome determination." Judge Ingram did stress the importance of mitigation evidence in making his "outcome determination," but it is clear that his predictive judgment rested on his assessment of the totality of the omitted evidence rather than on the notion that a single item of omitted evidence, no matter how trivial, would require a new hearing.

The Virginia Supreme Court's own analysis of prejudice reaching the contrary conclusion was thus unreasonable in at least two respects. First, as we have already explained, the State Supreme Court mischaracterized at best the appropriate rule, made clear by this Court in *Strickland*, for determining whether counsel's assistance was effective within the meaning of the Constitution. While it may also have conducted an "outcome determinative" analysis of its own, it is evident to us that the court's decision turned on its erroneous view that a "mere" difference in outcome is not sufficient to establish constitutionally ineffective assistance of counsel. Its analysis in this respect was thus not only "contrary to," but also, inasmuch as the Virginia Supreme Court relied on the inapplicable exception recognized in *Lockhart*, an "unreasonable application of" the clear law as established by this Court.

Second, the State Supreme Court's prejudice determination was unreasonable insofar as it failed to evaluate the totality of the available mitigation evidence—both that adduced at trial, and the evidence adduced in the habeas proceeding—in reweighing it against the evidence in aggravation. This error is apparent in its consideration of the additional mitigation evidence developed in the postconviction proceedings. The court correctly found that as to "the factual part of the mixed question," there was "really * * * n[o] * * * dispute" that available mitigation evidence was not presented at trial. As to the prejudice determination comprising the "legal part" of its analysis, it correctly emphasized the strength of the prosecution evidence supporting the future dangerousness aggravating circumstance.

But the state court failed even to mention the sole argument in mitigation that trial counsel did advance—Williams turned himself in, alerting police to a crime they otherwise would never have discovered, expressing remorse for his actions, and cooperating with the police after that. While this, coupled with the prison records and guard testimony, may not have overcome a finding of future dangerousness, the graphic description of Williams' childhood, filled with abuse and privation, or the reality that he was "borderline mentally retarded," might well have influenced the jury's appraisal of his moral culpability. The circumstances recited in his several confessions are consistent with the view that in each case his violent behavior was a compulsive reaction rather than the product of cold-blooded premeditation. Mitigating evidence unrelated to dangerousness may alter the jury's selection of penalty, even if it does not undermine or rebut the prosecution's death-eligibility case. The Virginia Supreme Court did not entertain that possibility. It thus failed to accord appropriate weight to the body of mitigation evidence available to trial counsel.

V

In our judgment, the state trial judge was correct both in his recognition of the established legal standard for determining counsel's effectiveness, and in his conclusion that the entire postconviction record, viewed as a whole and cumulative of mitigation evidence presented originally, raised "a reasonable probability that the result of the sentencing proceeding would have been different" if competent counsel had presented and explained the significance of all the available evidence. It follows that the Virginia Supreme Court rendered a "decision that was contrary to, or involved an unreasonable application of, clearly established Federal law." Williams' constitutional right to the effective assistance of counsel as defined in *Strickland* was violated.

Accordingly, the judgment of the Court of Appeals is reversed, and the case is remanded for further proceedings consistent with this opinion.

It is so ordered.

JUSTICE O'CONNOR delivered the opinion of the Court with respect to Part II (except as to the footnote), concurred in part, and concurred in the judgment.*

* * * The relevant provision prohibits a federal court from granting an application for a writ of habeas corpus with respect to a claim adjudicated on the merits in state court unless that adjudication "resulted in a decision that was contrary to, or involved an unreasonable application of, clearly established Federal law, as determined by the Supreme Court of the United States." The Court holds today that the Virginia Supreme Court's adjudication of Terry Williams' application for state habeas corpus relief resulted in just such a decision. I agree with that determination and join Parts I, III, and IV of the Court's opinion. Because I disagree, however, with the interpretation of § 2254(d)(1) set forth in Part II of Justice Stevens' opinion, I write separately to explain my views.

I

Before 1996, this Court held that a federal court entertaining a state prisoner's application for habeas relief must exercise its independent judgment when deciding both questions of constitutional law and mixed constitutional questions (*i.e.*, application of constitutional law to fact). In other words, a federal habeas court owed no deference to a state court's resolution of such questions of law or mixed questions. In * * * *Wright v. West*, we revisited our prior holdings by asking the parties to address the following question in their briefs:

> In determining whether to grant a petition for writ of habeas corpus by a person in custody pursuant to the judgment of a state court, should a federal court give deference to the state court's application of law to the specific facts of the petitioner's case or should it review the state court's determination *de novo*?" Although our ultimate decision did not turn on the answer to that question, our several opinions did join issue on it.

Justice Thomas, announcing the judgment of the Court, acknowledged that our precedents had "treat[ed] as settled the rule that mixed constitutional ques-

---

* Justice Kennedy joins this opinion in its entirety. The Chief Justice and Justice Thomas join this opinion with respect to Part II. Justice Scalia joins this opinion with respect to Part II, except as to the footnote.

tions are 'subject to plenary federal review' on habeas." He contended, nevertheless, that those decisions did not foreclose the Court from applying a rule of deferential review for reasonableness in future cases. According to Justice Thomas, the reliance of our precedents on *Brown v. Allen* was erroneous because the Court in *Brown* never explored in detail whether a federal habeas court, to deny a state prisoner's application, must conclude that the relevant state-court adjudication was "correct" or merely that it was "reasonable." Justice Thomas suggested that the time to revisit our decisions may have been at hand, given that our more recent habeas jurisprudence in the nonretroactivity context, *see, e.g., Teague v. Lane*, had called into question the then-settled rule of independent review of mixed constitutional questions.

I wrote separately in *Wright* because I believed Justice Thomas had "understate[d] the certainty with which *Brown v. Allen* rejected a deferential standard of review of issues of law." I also explained that we had considered the standard of review applicable to mixed constitutional questions on numerous occasions and each time we concluded that federal habeas courts had a duty to evaluate such questions independently. * * *

* * * Under the federal habeas statute as it stood in 1992, then, our precedents dictated that a federal court should grant a state prisoner's petition for habeas relief if that court were to conclude in its independent judgment that the relevant state court had erred on a question of constitutional law or on a mixed constitutional question.

If today's case were governed by the federal habeas statute prior to Congress' enactment of AEDPA in 1996, I would agree with Justice Stevens that Williams' petition for habeas relief must be granted if we, in our independent judgment, were to conclude that his Sixth Amendment right to effective assistance of counsel was violated.

II

A

Williams' case is *not* governed by the pre-1996 version of the habeas statute. Because he filed his petition in December 1997, Williams' case is governed by the statute as amended by AEDPA. * * *

Accordingly, for Williams to obtain federal habeas relief, he must first demonstrate that his case satisfies the condition set by § 2254(d)(1). That provision modifies the role of federal habeas courts in reviewing petitions filed by state prisoners.

Justice Stevens' opinion in Part II essentially contends that § 2254(d)(1) does not alter the previously settled rule of independent review. Indeed, the opinion concludes its statutory inquiry with the somewhat empty finding that § 2254(d)(1) does no more than express a " 'mood' that the federal judiciary must respect." For Justice Stevens, the congressionally enacted "mood" has two important qualities. First, "federal courts [must] attend to every state-court judgment with utmost care" by "carefully weighing all the reasons for accepting a state court's judgment." Second, if a federal court undertakes that careful review and yet remains convinced that a prisoner's custody violates the Constitution, "that independent judgment should prevail."

* * * Justice Stevens' interpretation of § 2254(d)(1) gives the 1996 amendment no effect whatsoever. The command that federal courts should now use the "utmost care" by "carefully weighing" the reasons supporting a state court's judgment echoes our pre-AEDPA statement * * * that federal habeas courts "should, of course, give great weight to the considered conclusions of a coequal state judiciary." Similarly, the requirement that the independent judgment of a federal court must in the end prevail essentially repeats the conclusion we reached in the very next sentence * * * with respect to the specific issue presented there: "But, as we now reaffirm, the ultimate question whether, under the totality of the circumstances, the challenged confession was obtained in a manner compatible with the requirements of the Constitution *is a matter for independent federal determination.*" ([E]mphasis added).

That Justice Stevens would find the new § 2254(d)(1) to have no effect on the prior law of habeas corpus is remarkable given his apparent acknowledgment that Congress wished to bring change to the field. That acknowledgment is correct and significant to this case. It cannot be disputed that Congress viewed § 2254(d)(1) as an important means by which its goals for habeas reform would be achieved.

Justice Stevens arrives at his erroneous interpretation by means of one critical misstep. He fails to give independent meaning to both the "contrary to" and "unreasonable application" clauses of the statute. By reading § 2254(d)(1) as one general restriction on the power of the federal habeas court, Justice Stevens manages to avoid confronting the specific meaning of the statute's "unreasonable application" clause and its ramifications for the independent-review rule. It is, however, a cardinal principle of statutory construction that we must " 'give effect, if possible, to every clause and word of a statute.' " Section 2254(d)(1) defines two categories of cases in which a state prisoner may obtain federal habeas relief with respect to a claim adjudicated on the merits in state court[:] * * * if the relevant state-court decision was either (1) "*contrary to* * * * clearly established Federal law, as determined by the Supreme Court of the United States," or (2) "*involved an unreasonable application of* * * * clearly established Federal law, as determined by the Supreme Court of the United States." (Emphases added.)

The Court of Appeals for the Fourth Circuit properly accorded both the "contrary to" and "unreasonable application" clauses independent meaning. * * * With respect to the first of the two statutory clauses, the Fourth Circuit held in *Green* that a state-court decision can be "contrary to" this Court's clearly established precedent in two ways. First, a state-court decision is contrary to this Court's precedent if the state court arrives at a conclusion opposite to that reached by this Court on a question of law. Second, a state-court decision is also contrary to this Court's precedent if the state court confronts facts that are materially indistinguishable from a relevant Supreme Court precedent and arrives at a result opposite to ours.

The word "contrary" is commonly understood to mean "diametrically different," "opposite in character or nature," or "mutually opposed." The text of

§ 2254(d)(1) therefore suggests that the state court's decision must be substantially different from the relevant precedent of this Court. The Fourth Circuit's interpretation of the "contrary to" clause accurately reflects this textual meaning. A state-court decision will certainly be contrary to our clearly established precedent if the state court applies a rule that contradicts the governing law set forth in our cases. * * * A state-court decision will also be contrary to this Court's clearly established precedent if the state court confronts a set of facts that are materially indistinguishable from a decision of this Court and nevertheless arrives at a result different from our precedent. Accordingly, in either of these two scenarios, a federal court will be unconstrained by § 2254(d)(1) because the state-court decision falls within that provision's "contrary to" clause.

On the other hand, a run-of-the-mill state-court decision applying the correct legal rule from our cases to the facts of a prisoner's case would not fit comfortably within § 2254(d)(1)'s "contrary to" clause. Assume, for example, that a state-court decision on a prisoner's ineffective-assistance claim correctly identifies *Strickland* as the controlling legal authority and, applying that framework, rejects the prisoner's claim. Quite clearly, the state-court decision would be in accord with our decision in *Strickland* as to the legal prerequisites for establishing an ineffective-assistance claim, even assuming the federal court considering the prisoner's habeas application might reach a different result applying the *Strickland* framework itself. It is difficult, however, to describe such a run-of-the-mill state-court decision as "diametrically different" from, "opposite in character or nature" from, or "mutually opposed" to *Strickland*, our clearly established precedent. Although the state-court decision may be contrary to the federal court's conception of how *Strickland* ought to be applied in that particular case, the decision is not "mutually opposed" to *Strickland* itself.

Justice Stevens would instead construe § 2254(d)(1)'s "contrary to" clause to encompass such a routine state-court decision. That construction, however, saps the "unreasonable application" clause of any meaning. If a federal habeas court can, under the "contrary to" clause, issue the writ whenever it concludes that the state court's *application* of clearly established federal law was incorrect, the "unreasonable application" clause becomes a nullity. We must, however, if possible, give meaning to every clause of the statute. Justice Stevens not only makes no attempt to do so, but also construes the "contrary to" clause in a manner that ensures that the "unreasonable application" clause will have no independent meaning. We reject that expansive interpretation of the statute. Reading § 2254(d)(1)'s "contrary to" clause to permit a federal court to grant relief in cases where a state court's error is limited to the manner in which it *applies* Supreme Court precedent is suspect given the logical and natural fit of the neighboring "unreasonable application" clause to such cases.

The Fourth Circuit's interpretation of the "unreasonable application" clause of § 2254(d)(1) is generally correct. That court held in *Green* that a state-court decision can involve an "unreasonable application" of this Court's clearly established precedent in two ways. First, a state-court decision involves an unreasonable application of this Court's precedent if the state court identifies the correct governing legal rule from this Court's cases but unreasonably applies it to the facts of the particular state prisoner's case. Second, a state-court decision also involves an unreasonable application of this Court's precedent if the state court either unreasonably extends a legal principle from our precedent to a new context where it should not apply or unreasonably refuses to extend that principle to a new context where it should apply.

A state-court decision that correctly identifies the governing legal rule but applies it unreasonably to the facts of a particular prisoner's case certainly would qualify as a decision "involv[ing] an unreasonable application of * * * clearly established Federal law." Indeed, we used the almost identical phrase "application of law" to describe a state court's application of law to fact in the certiorari question we posed to the parties in *Wright*.*

The Fourth Circuit also held in *Green* that state-court decisions that unreasonably extend a legal principle from our precedent to a new context where it should not apply (or unreasonably refuse to extend a legal principle to a new context where it should apply) should be analyzed under § 2254(d)(1)'s "unreasonable application" clause. Although that holding may perhaps be correct, the classification does have some problems of precision. Just as it is sometimes difficult to distinguish a mixed question of law and fact from a question of fact, it will often be difficult to identify separately those state-court decisions that involve an unreasonable application of a legal principle (or an unreasonable failure to apply a legal principle) to a new context. Indeed, on the one hand, in some cases it will be hard to distinguish a decision involving an unreasonable extension of a legal principle from a decision involving an unreasonable application of law to facts. On the other hand, in many of the same cases it will also be difficult to distinguish a decision involving an unreasonable extension of a legal principle from a decision that "arrives at a conclusion opposite to that reached by this Court on a question of law." Today's case does not require us to decide how such "extension of legal principle" cases should be treated under § 2254(d)(1). For now it is sufficient to hold that when a state-court decision unreasonably applies the law of this Court to the facts of a prisoner's case, a federal court applying § 2254(d)(1) may conclude that the state-court decision falls within that provision's "unreasonable application" clause.

B

There remains the task of defining what exactly qualifies as an "unreasonable application" of law under § 2254(d)(1). The Fourth Circuit held in Green that a state-court decision involves an "unreasonable application of * * * clearly established Federal law" only if the state court has applied federal law "in a manner that reasonable jurists would all agree is unreasonable." The placement of this additional overlay on the "unreasonable application" clause was erroneous.

---

* The legislative history of § 2254(d)(1) also supports this interpretation. ("[U]nder the bill deference will be owed to State courts' decisions on the application of Federal law to the facts. Unless it is unreasonable, a State court's decision applying the law to the facts will be upheld"); ("[W]e allow a Federal court to overturn a State court decision only if it is contrary to clearly established Federal law or if it involves an 'unreasonable application' of clearly established Federal law to the facts").

It is difficult to fault the Fourth Circuit for using this language given the fact that we have employed nearly identical terminology to describe the related inquiry undertaken by federal courts in applying the nonretroactivity rule of *Teague*. * * *

Defining an "unreasonable application" by reference to a "reasonable jurist," however, is of little assistance to the courts that must apply § 2254(d)(1) and, in fact, may be misleading. Stated simply, a federal habeas court making the "unreasonable application" inquiry should ask whether the state court's application of clearly established federal law was objectively unreasonable. The federal habeas court should not transform the inquiry into a subjective one by resting its determination instead on the simple fact that at least one of the Nation's jurists has applied the relevant federal law in the same manner the state court did in the habeas petitioner's case. The "all reasonable jurists" standard would tend to mislead federal habeas courts by focusing their attention on a subjective inquiry rather than on an objective one. * * * As I explained in *Wright* with respect to the "reasonable jurist" standard in the *Teague* context, "[e]ven though we have characterized the new rule inquiry as whether 'reasonable jurists' could disagree as to whether a result is dictated by precedent, the standard for determining when a case establishes a new rule is 'objective,' and the mere existence of conflicting authority does not necessarily mean a rule is new."

The term "unreasonable" is no doubt difficult to define. That said, it is a common term in the legal world and, accordingly, federal judges are familiar with its meaning. For purposes of today's opinion, the most important point is that an *unreasonable* application of federal law is different from an *incorrect* application of federal law. Our opinions in *Wright*, for example, make that difference clear. Justice Thomas' criticism of this Court's subsequent reliance on *Brown* turned on that distinction. The Court in *Brown*, Justice Thomas contended, held only that a federal habeas court must determine whether the relevant state-court adjudication resulted in a " 'satisfactory conclusion.' " In Justice Thomas' view, *Brown* did not answer "the question whether a 'satisfactory' conclusion was one that the habeas court considered correct, as opposed to merely *reasonable*." ([E]mphases in original). In my separate opinion in *Wright*, I made the same distinction, maintaining that "a state court's *incorrect* legal determination has [never] been allowed to stand because it was *reasonable*. We have always held that federal courts, even on habeas, have an independent obligation to say what the law is." ([E]mphases added). In § 2254(d)(1), Congress specifically used the word "unreasonable," and not a term like "erroneous" or "incorrect." Under § 2254(d)(1)'s "unreasonable application" clause, then, a federal habeas court may not issue the writ simply because that court concludes in its independent judgment that the relevant state-court decision applied clearly established federal law erroneously or incorrectly. Rather, that application must also be unreasonable.

Justice Stevens turns a blind eye to the debate in *Wright* because he finds no indication in § 2254(d)(1) itself that Congress was "directly influenced" by Justice Thomas' opinion in *Wright*. As Justice Stevens himself apparently recognizes, however, Congress need not mention a prior decision of this Court by name in a statute's text in order to adopt either a rule or a meaning given a certain term in that decision. In any event, whether Congress intended to codify the standard of review suggested by Justice Thomas in *Wright* is beside the point. *Wright* is important for the light it sheds on § 2254(d)(1)'s requirement that a federal habeas court inquire into the reasonableness of a state court's application of clearly established federal law. The separate opinions in *Wright* concerned the very issue addressed by § 2254(d)(1)'s "unreasonable application" clause—whether, in reviewing a state-court decision on a state prisoner's claims under federal law, a federal habeas court should ask whether the state-court decision was correct or simply whether it was reasonable. Justice Stevens' claim that the debate in *Wright* concerned only the meaning of the *Teague* nonretroactivity rule is simply incorrect. As even a cursory review of Justice Thomas' opinion and my own opinion reveals, both the broader debate and the specific statements to which we refer concerned precisely the issue of the standard of review to be employed by federal habeas courts. The *Wright* opinions confirm what § 2254(d)(1)'s language already makes clear—that an *unreasonable* application of federal law is different from an *incorrect* or *erroneous* application of federal law.

Throughout this discussion the meaning of the phrase "clearly established Federal law, as determined by the Supreme Court of the United States" has been put to the side. That statutory phrase refers to the holdings, as opposed to the *dicta*, of this Court's decisions as of the time of the relevant state-court decision. In this respect, the "clearly established Federal law" phrase bears only a slight connection to our *Teague* jurisprudence. With one caveat, whatever would qualify as an old rule under our *Teague* jurisprudence will constitute "clearly established Federal law, as determined by the Supreme Court of the United States" under § 2254(d)(1). The one caveat, as the statutory language makes clear, is that § 2254(d)(1) restricts the source of clearly established law to this Court's jurisprudence.

In sum, § 2254(d)(1) places a new constraint on the power of a federal habeas court to grant a state prisoner's application for a writ of habeas corpus with respect to claims adjudicated on the merits in state court. Under § 2254(d)(1), the writ may issue only if one of the following two conditions is satisfied—the state-court adjudication resulted in a decision that (1) "was contrary to * * * clearly established Federal law, as determined by the Supreme Court of the United States," or (2) "involved an unreasonable application of * * * clearly established Federal law, as determined by the Supreme Court of the United States." Under the "contrary to" clause, a federal habeas court may grant the writ if the state court arrives at a conclusion opposite to that reached by this Court on a question of law or if the state court decides a case differently than this Court has on a set of materially indistinguishable facts. Under the "unreasonable application" clause, a federal habeas court may grant the writ if the state court identifies the correct governing legal principle from this Court's decisions but unreasonably applies that principle to the facts of the prisoner's case.

III

Although I disagree with Justice Stevens concerning the standard we must apply under § 2254(d)(1) in evaluating Terry Williams' claims on habeas, I agree with the Court that the Virginia Supreme Court's adjudication of Williams' claim of ineffective assistance of counsel resulted in a decision that was both contrary to and involved an unreasonable application of this Court's clearly established precedent. Specifically, I believe that the Court's discussion in Parts III and IV is correct and that it demonstrates the reasons that the Virginia Supreme Court's decision in Williams' case, even under the interpretation of § 2254(d)(1) I have set forth above, was both contrary to and involved an unreasonable application of our precedent.

* * *

To be sure, as The Chief Justice notes, the Virginia Supreme Court did also inquire whether Williams had demonstrated a reasonable probability that, but for his trial counsel's unprofessional errors, the result of his sentencing would have been different. It is impossible to determine, however, the extent to which the Virginia Supreme Court's error with respect to its reading of Lockhart affected its ultimate finding that Williams suffered no prejudice. For example, at the conclusion of its discussion of whether Williams had demonstrated a reasonable probability of a different outcome at sentencing, the Virginia Supreme Court faulted the Virginia Circuit Court for its "emphasis on mere outcome determination, without proper attention to whether the result of the criminal proceeding was fundamentally unfair or unreliable." As the Court explains, however, Williams' case did not implicate the unusual circumstances present in cases like *Lockhart* or *Nix v. Whiteside*. Accordingly, for the very reasons I set forth in my *Lockhart* concurrence, the emphasis on outcome was entirely appropriate in Williams' case.

Third, I also agree with the Court that, to the extent the Virginia Supreme Court did apply Strickland, its application was unreasonable. * * * The Virginia Supreme Court's decision reveals an obvious failure to consider the totality of the omitted mitigation evidence. For that reason, and the remaining factors discussed in the Court's opinion, I believe that the Virginia Supreme Court's decision "involved an unreasonable application of * * * clearly established Federal law, as determined by the Supreme Court of the United States."

Accordingly, although I disagree with the interpretation of § 2254(d)(1) set forth in Part II of Justice Stevens' opinion, I join Parts I, III, and IV of the Court's opinion and concur in the judgment of reversal.

[Chief Justice Rehnquist, joined by Justices Scalia and Thomas, agreed with the Court's analytical framework as set out in Justice Stevens's and O'Connor's opinions. They diverged, however, from the Court's conclusion that the omitted evidence might have changed the result, finding as a practical matter that the omission was similar to harmless error.]

Notes and Questions

1. The prejudice inquiry demanded by the Court's jurisprudence may cause a court to say, as the Fourth Circuit did here, that although the state courts committed constitutional error, their decision must nonetheless stand because the federal court concludes

that the outcome of the state proceeding would not have been altered had the state court proceeding been untainted. Does that amount to harmless error analysis? If so, is it appropriate in a case where the federal court is attempting to forecast what an unreviewable jury decision would be? After all, if the case (or in this instance the sentencing part of the case) were retried and the jury declined to recommend the death penalty, the trial court could not set the jury's decision aside, nor could the prosecution appeal it. Consider whether, if the sentencing phase took place again but without the constitutional error (here ineffective assistance of counsel), the trial court could direct the jury to bring in a recommendation for the death penalty.

2. What exactly was the problem with the Fourth Circuit's approach to *Strickland*? Was it an unreasonable reading of *Strickland*?

3. a) Should federal courts defer at all to state interpretations of federal law? Justice Stevens thinks not. Does Justice O'Connor differ in this respect? If so, how? If not, then why was she unable to join Part II of Justice Stevens's opinion?

b) Assume that Congress indeed intended to codify a rule of deference by federal courts to the opinions of state courts on federal law. Is that permissible, or does it violate separation of powers by intruding on the judicial function? Could Congress in effect adopt the approach to state adjudication of federal issues that Virginia urged in *Martin v. Hunter's Lessee*, thus making impossible Supreme Court review of state court decisions on federal constitutional matters?

c) Still with respect to the authoritativeness of federal courts in the area of federal law, does or should their authoritativeness differ according to whether they are reviewing a pure statement of federal law by the state courts or application of federal law to the facts? If so, why are they less authoritative on one area than the other? If not, then what are we to make of the two phrases in 28 U.S.C. § 2254(d)(1) that lie at the heart of this case: "contrary to" and "unreasonable application of"?

4. a) Is it a fair characterization to read "contrary to" as "wrong as a matter of law"? That is Justice Stevens's position. If that is correct, how can we explain Congress choosing to codify pre-existing law but nonetheless opting for different language? If it is not correct, then what is the difference between the two phrases?

b) Is Justice Stevens correct that *Marbury v. Madison* compels a "simply wrong" standard, or is *Marbury* distinguishable?

5. a) Justice Stevens says that "clearly established" is a federal question. If the federal courts find that a rule is not clearly established, how will it ever become so? Pursuant to § 2254(d)(1), even the Supreme Court cannot order habeas relief if the federal rule was not clearly established. Has Congress effectively put a "cap" on the scope of federal rights to which a state prisoner is entitled?

b) Section 2254(d)(1) now clearly limits the source of federal constitutional law binding on the states to the Supreme Court. Does that effectively put pressure on the Court to accept for review cases in which the Circuits are unanimous (and in the Court's view correct) about the existence of a particular constitutional rule, or has that category simply ceased to exist under the new statutory structure?

6. a) Justice Stevens thinks that the statutory phrases "contrary to" and "unreasonable application of" are not mutually exclusive. Justice O'Connor thinks they are (and has the majority to prove it). If you were on the Court, how would you vote? Why?

b) Is Justice O'Connor correct in charging that Justice Stevens's reading of the statute leaves nothing for the "unreasonable application" language to do? Note that she endorses the Fourth Circuit's categorization of the kinds of cases that will fall under the two phrases. It is interesting to juxtapose them without the statutory labels:

> First, a state-court decision is contrary to this Court's precedent if the state court arrives at a conclusion opposite to that reached by this Court on a question of law. Second, a state-court decision is also contrary to this Court's precedent if the state court confronts facts that are materially indistinguishable from a relevant Supreme Court precedent and arrives at a result opposite to ours.
>
> * * *
>
> [Third,] a state-court decision involves an unreasonable application of this Court's precedent if the state court identifies the correct governing legal rule from this Court's cases but unreasonably applies it to the facts of the particular state prisoner's case. [Fourth,] a state-court decision also involves an unreasonable application of this Court's precedent if the state court either unreasonably extends a legal principle from our precedent to a new context where it should not apply or unreasonably refuses to extend that principle to a new context where it should apply.

How different are the second and third categories? If the state court confronts materially indistinguishable facts and reaches that an opposite result, is that different from a state court using the correct rule but unreasonably applying it to the facts? How can we know that the state court application is unreasonable save by comparing the state case with the facts of the Supreme Court case that announced the rule (and perhaps other Supreme Court cases that elaborated it)? If you think that they are not different, can you construct cases that would satisfy one but not the other? Is it also possible that there are cases that satisfy both?

To the extent that you feel that those two categories do overlap, does that give some support, however unintended, to Justice Stevens's view that the two statutory phrases do overlap? Assuming for the moment that they do, does the fourth category nonetheless give "unreasonable application of" something to do, perhaps undercutting Justice O'Connor's criticism of Justice Stevens's approach?

c) Justice O'Connor takes the position that "unreasonable" is something more than incorrect. What does she think is the difference between the two? Note that she does not offer an example of a wrong-but-reasonable application. Can you hypothesize one?

7. What do you think of the good-faith standard for which some of the *amici* argued? Does it somehow convert the constitutional principles that might be involved in a particular case from rights of the defendant to a simple restraint on malicious courts? Does it have a tendency to make constitutional law whatever state judges think it is, so long as they think it in good faith? If so, what has happened to the authoritativeness of the law, particularly law "clearly established by the Supreme Court"?

To be inserted on page 1013 immediately before Note 2 d):

Fiore v. White, 531 U.S. 225, 121 S.Ct. 712, 148 L.Ed.2d 629 (2001), demonstrates that the federal courts still encounter difficulty in figuring out when the state courts have announced a "new" rule. The Pennsylvania courts convicted Fiore of operating a hazardous waste facility without a permit. The trial court accepted the state's argument that Fiore had so grossly overstepped the limitations of the permit he held that he effectively was operating without a permit. The intermediate appellate court affirmed, and the Pennsylvania Supreme Court declined to review the case. That court later did review and reverse the conviction of Fiore's co-defendant, ruling that the statute's specification of operating *without* a permit precluded conviction for violating a permit's terms, no matter how egregiously. Fiore thereupon sought state collateral relief and, when unsuccessful, brought a habeas petition to the federal courts. The United States Court of Appeals for the Third Circuit reversed the district court's grant of the writ in the belief that Pennsylvania's Supreme Court had announced a new rule of law not applicable to Fiore. The United States Supreme Court reversed in a *per curiam* decision. It did so because it had certified to the Pennsylvania Supreme Court the question of whether that court's interpretation of the statute in the later case "state[d] the correct interpretation of the law of Pennsylvania at the date Fiore's conviction became final * * *." The Pennsylvania Supreme Court replied that it did and that the case "did not announce a new rule of law. Our ruling merely clarified the plain language of the statute * * *." Note the confusion on all three levels of federal courts. The District Court, granting habeas relief, felt that the rule was clearly not new within the meaning of *Teague*. The Court of Appeals felt that it clearly was. The United States Supreme Court declined to guess.

To be inserted on page 1014 immediately before Note 2 e):

Tyler v. Cain, ___ U.S. ___, ___ S.Ct. ___, ___ L.Ed.2d ___, 2001 WL 720703 (June 28, 2001), may have made it even more difficult for a state prisoner to take advantage of a new constitutional rule that the Supreme Court has recognized. A jury had convicted Tyler of second-degree murder upon an instruction relating to the meaning of "proof beyond a reasonable doubt" that the Court later found unconstitutional in its *per curiam* decision in *Cage v. Louisiana*, 498 U.S. 39, 111 S.Ct. 328, 112 L.Ed.2d 339 (1990). That decision alone did not make the new rule retroactive, but in *Sullivan v. Louisiana*, 508 U.S. 275, 113 S.Ct. 2078, 124 L.Ed.2d 182 (1993), the Court held that the *Cage* rule was structural, not subject to harmless-error analysis and would "always invalidate the conviction." Tyler argued that the *Cage-Sullivan* combination "made" the *Cage* rule retroactive within the meaning of AEDPA, § 2244(b)(1)(A). The Court's five-member majority disagreed: "Based on the plain meaning of the text read as a whole, we conclude that 'made' means 'held' and, thus, the requirement is satisfied only if this Court has held that the new rule is retroactively applicable to cases on collateral review." Justice Thomas's opinion then noted that neither *Cage* nor *Sullivan* so held, and that "[m]ultiple cases can render a new rule retroactive only if the holdings in those cases necessarily dictate retroactivity of the new rule." Dissenting, Justice Breyer, joined by Justices Stevens, Souter and Ginsburg, argued that the majority misread the statute to require a formal holding by the Court and that in any event, the *Cage-Sullivan* duo made clear that the *Cage* rule was retroactive under the Court's long-existing standards for retroactivity.

The majority also noted that

[b]ecause Tyler's habeas application was his second, the District Court was required to dismiss it unless Tyler showed that this Court already had made Cage retroactive. * * * We cannot decide today whether *Cage* is retroactive to cases on collateral review, because that distinction would not help Tyler in this case. Any statement on *Cage*'s retroactivity would be *dictum*, so we decline to comment further on the issue.

Query, after *Tyler*, how a rule can become retroactive. The Court that announces the rule cannot simultaneously make it retroactive; that would be *dictum* under Justice Thomas's analysis. If the Court in *Tyler* cannot do so either, has the Court foreclosed all possibility of the rule being declared retroactive? Not necessarily; a prisoner presenting his first federal habeas application and therefore not facing the additional hurdles that confront someone submitted a second or subsequent petition may seek such a holding. Note, however, that this presents again the possible anomaly of prisoners convicted of the same offense at the same trial on the same jury instruction having their fate determined by the speed with which their appeals and state post-conviction remedies run. If one prisoner's first federal habeas application antedates the announcement of the new rule's retroactivity and the other postdates it, only the latter's second federal habeas petition will result in relief.

G. EXHAUSTION OF REMEDIES

To be inserted on page 1026 immediately before Note 11:

Slack v. McDaniel, 529 U.S. 473, 120 S.Ct. 1595, 146 L.Ed.2d 542 (2000), elaborated a bit on the treatment of mixed petitions under AEDPA. Slack had filed an original federal habeas petition that contained exhausted and unexhausted claims. He asked the district court to hold his action in abeyance while he exhausted his remaining claims in the state courts. The court instead dismissed the petition without prejudice, noting specifically that Slack was entitled to renew the petition after exhausting his state remedies. When Slack refiled a petition containing all of the original claims and some new ones, the state objected, arguing that the inclusion of new claims made the petition a "second or successive petition" that constituted abuse of the writ. The district court dismissed the new claims. The Ninth Circuit affirmed that action, but also dismissed the remainder of the petition on *Rose v. Lundy* grounds. The Supreme Court reversed, holding that "[a] habeas petition filed in the district court after an initial habeas petition was unadjudicated on its merits and dismissed for failure to exhaust state remedies is not a second or successive petition." *Lundy*, said the Court, intended only to avoid piecemeal adjudication; here the prisoner had done exactly what *Lundy* contemplated. Justices Scalia and Thomas dissented from the part of the Court's holding that allowed the inclusion of the new claims. Note the bind in which their interpretation of *Lundy* puts the prisoner. What is the dilemma that he faces?